LEAP

LEAP

MAKING THE JUMP TO TAKE NETBALL TO THE TOP OF THE WORLD

GEVA MENTOR

WITH ABI SMITH

CORONET

First published in Great Britain in 2019 by Coronet
An Imprint of Hodder & Stoughton
An Hachette UK company

This paperback edition published in 2020

1

A CIP catalogue record for this title is available from the British Library

Paperback ISBN 9781529353389
eBook ISBN 9781529353365

Typeset in Minion Pro by
Palimpsest Book Production Ltd, Falkirk, Stirlingshire

Printed and bound in Great Britain by Clays Ltd, Elcograf S.p.A.

Hodder & Stoughton policy is to use papers that are natural, renewable
and recyclable products and made from wood grown in sustainable forests.
The logging and manufacturing processes are expected to conform to the
environmental regulations of the country of origin.

Hodder & Stoughton Ltd
Carmelite House
50 Victoria Embankment
London EC4Y 0DZ

www.hodder.co.uk

To all the unique people, who dare to
be different, continually pay it forward
and whose innuendos are top notch!

CONTENTS

PROLOGUE

'While I'm loath to make comparisons between great athletes, to give you some idea of her influence and standing in women's sporting circles, Geva is to netball as Roger Federer is to tennis.'

Jenny Sinclair, managing editor, *Netball Scoop*

A BOOK? Really, Mum? Me, write a book?'

'Think about it, Geev, you've had one hell of a year, 2018 has been a rollercoaster of a ride. The stuff that has happened this year alone would be enough to write about – three awards, two trophies, one divorce . . .'

The word hung in the air as she looked at me. 'What I mean is, why not tell people everything. Everything that thirty years of being involved in sport has culminated in – this incredible professional year on court coinciding with a heartbreaking personal one off court. Be honest and show folks what hard work and dedication and sacrifice looks like. Sing it from the rooftops, so women and men, girls and boys can see what can be achieved with a positive attitude and self-belief. It's just a suggestion. But you should do it.'

Mum was right. Like mums normally are. The year 2018 had been one of incredible highs and some heartbreaking lows. And the more I thought about it, the more her idea didn't seem so crazy. I had recently become an ambassador for the JAN Trust, empowering Black, African, Minority and Ethnic women (BAME) in communities to achieve their full potential. A book was on a bigger scale but it would have the same message: that my experience might benefit others. That the path I have trodden might well resonate with someone and then someone else and the legacy of hard work and commitment and focus would continue.

I do receive lots of wonderful messages from young girls and women telling me I inspire them and I am their idol and, as lovely as it is to hear, I can't get my head round that concept at all. An idol? Me? Are they sure?! I have never really had an idol so I can't really fathom that.

'You're such an inspiration, I want to be just like you, I love watching you play,' they say. And 'My daughter really looks up to you, she wants to be just like you.' I don't know how to reply or what to say. It's easy when they ask me for playing tips or advice; my response to those sorts of questions come very easily – but not when I am called an inspiration. How would you respond? I feel like a phoney sometimes as I don't always eat healthily, I don't always feel like training and I can be quite stubborn. But perhaps that is what makes me relatable and normal. An inspiration? I'm just me. Geva Mentor. But I suppose in a sense it is quite reassuring that what I am doing is making a bit of a difference, having a positive impact on people. I'm just going about my normal business, I'm just playing netball. Netball has been my business for nearly twenty years, so you could say I have shown commitment to it for sure. I have dedicated myself to it, yes; but I didn't set out to. Not in the beginning. I often say netball found me, I didn't find it – there was a heap of other things I was doing before netball came into my life.

Before I moved to Australia to improve my game.

Before I got signed up for the England senior squad.

Before I got picked for the England under-twenty-one squad.

Before I got scouted for the England under-seventeen team.

Before playing for a county, a club, a school . . .

Back in the beginning netball was probably the furthest thing from my mind.

'What would you be doing if you weren't a netballer?' I get asked that A LOT. Probably every interview I have ever done, people ask me that.

What did I want to be when I was growing up? I struggle to answer that, even to this day. I think I just used to make things up when I would get asked those questions in interviews for TV or magazines. Or I'd say whatever popped into my mind at that moment.

I never really had any professional objectives, I never had a set career path. When I was younger I think my 'plan', such as it was, was just to be healthy and happy and enjoy whatever I decided to do. I don't know if that makes me a bit different as it means I'm not driven in terms of wanting a certain career path – or maybe it is a positive as it means I have been able to just go with the flow. Don't get me wrong, that doesn't mean I haven't given things 100 per cent, but I'm a firm believer that if you enjoy what you are doing you'll put more into it. Rather than having a rigid plan, I have seen opportunities as they arise and taken them if I felt like it. I never set out to play netball, it was never on my radar; it was a case of just giving it a go. A bit like going to Australia. A bit like being a university student now, later in life, as I know now that I like working with kids, inspiring the next generation. And I have worked out where I feel most settled, where I best fit in. In a team, working as a team. So you see, I really, really struggle with the questions, What do you want to be when you grow up? and What would you be doing if you weren't a netballer? I guess what

I'm trying to say is, it's OK to not know. Sometimes you just have to take a leap of faith.

Aah, that word. Leap. The title of my book.

The word conjures up so many images, doesn't it? You've probably not thought too much about it, but to me that word means a great deal. I have taken leaps of faith throughout my life and my career. Sometimes I have found that to be my only mode of transport. Of course, I leap a lot in the literal sense too – I leap to take intercepts, block shots, to defend my post, to win games as that is what I do, that is my job. But I have found my life to have been a series of opportunities and challenges and I have leapt into the unknown on many occasions. I have worked bloody hard, but I have never lost the belief that everything will work out in the end. You have to have that belief, take that leap sometimes. Trust me, keep reading. You'll see what I mean . . .

1 SPRINGING
INTO ACTION

*'It was written in the stars, Geva Kate (G.K.), and little
did I know she would be playing GK for England.'*
Yvonne Mentor, mum

I PEEKED over the top of the green curtain; the solid green
base of it was meant to act as a privacy shield but I was
tall enough, if I stood on my tiptoes, to see above and
through the netting part of the curtain. I curled my fingers
round the netting and pressed my face up against the strings.
The springs of the trampoline beds were making a rhyth-
mical noise and the trampolinists bounced gracefully. I
watched in awe. They looked like they were flying, bounding
and leaping all over the place and having so much fun. I
had been doing gymnastics for a few weeks now and every
week I heard the noise of the trampolines and wished I was
the other side of the big green curtain. Everyone looked so
happy over there, everyone was smiling, chatting and having
a laugh. This is what I should be doing. I wanted to be over

that side of the curtain too. The funny thing was my mum was on that side – she was one of the trampolining instructors, coaching the athletes as they took turns on the trampolines. My mind was made up. Gymnastics was fun, don't get me wrong; it had given me a good understanding of core stability and discipline, but I had given it a go and now I wanted to try something else.

I was only ten years old but already the thought of trampolining was what I had my heart set on. Forget gymnastics . . . rocking up to train in shorts and a T-shirt? Yes please! I was a bit of a tomboy so this was extra-appealing. Bouncing high in the air and feeling a sense of weightlessness and freedom is hard to describe. I could often bounce high enough to peer over the balcony and see what was going on in the café, where I would check how long the line was for the Slush Puppie machine. That was a post-training treat I had negotiated with Mum!

I still get a little buzz now when I see a trampoline. The urge to jump on one is strong; however, I know people would freak out because of the risk of injury! I do have to be careful nowadays, although I reckon I could get on and do a few bounces – just maybe not the double somersaults. Although to be fair, I'm definitely not as fearless now as the ten-year-old me was. The ten-year-old me joined the trampolining classes the following week and although Mum wasn't my coach, we were now the same side of the curtain, both having fun.

* * *

Mum was pretty good at getting me to try different sports, and trampolining was no different. She didn't mind about gymnastics; she knew I had given it a go. She was a county tennis and squash player and so would take me down to the tennis courts for a hit-about. Sport was all around her when she was growing up and so it was natural for her to surround me with sports and activities. Her father was an athlete, her grandfather was a sailor and she was into tennis. So I loved anything sporty. And she was nearly in the Olympics too – well, sort of. Before I was born she was into windsurfing big time and, in the early eighties, it was awarded Olympic status. A couple of the other GB potentials went to Australia for their warm-weather winter training but Mum couldn't afford that, so she went to St Lucia instead after being offered a deal. And it was a good thing she did too as she met my dad there! It's so funny when she tells the story. She was twenty-three years old at the time and apparently didn't have time for boys until she saw my dad, Gregory, early on her first morning, coming out of the ocean. She had flown in the night before and couldn't sleep so went for an early morning run on the beach. He was working for the local hotel and would supply them with fresh fish he had caught with his spear gun. He emerged from the ocean, spear in one hand and catch in the other, dripping wet, a very tall, very muscly black man, and Mum was struck by love at first sight. He apparently was too as he spotted her – an athletic white woman training on the beach with a big smile – and, as the sun came up, they started talking. Mum says they talked so long that the fish he had caught spoiled in the sun and he was unable to sell them to the hotel. Dad says it was the best catch ever, too, but Mum was worth it. Mum says that was crap as she was his best catch ever! Mum never did much windsurfing training after that; she phoned my grandma and told her she was staying in the Caribbean for a few weeks longer and the rest, as they say, is history. My brother and I definitely take after our dad in terms of figure – he is very tall and athletic and has very long legs. Mum says she is bloody pleased we have both inherited his physique and not her short, dumpy legs – although she does point out that as she has a low centre of gravity she doesn't topple over very often. So there you have it.

Looking at them, you probably couldn't get two more different people: Dad, who is over six foot tall, a dark-skinned man-mountain, and Mum, an only child from a white English middle-class family. But it was love.

They got married in St Lucia and spent the first few years of married life, before I was born, enjoying a wonderful, free-spirit type of existence in the Caribbean. Mum says she remembers lying on the beach, pregnant with me, listening to an old-fashioned radio after a busy day of windsurfing. She knew she had to come back over to England to have me as back in the eighties there were problems with children being born out of the country to an English parent – potentially they might not be recognised as GB nationals. She was convinced I was going to be a girl, apparently; there were no names chosen for if I was a boy but she heard on the radio, on that warm Caribbean afternoon, an Indian opera singer who was visiting the island and performing. On that small, crackling radio, Mum thought they announced her name as Geva. She fell in love with the name. It was only years later that she discovered the opera singer was of Sri Lankan descent and her name was spelled and pronounced 'Jeeva', which means 'life'. Mum's spelling, Geva, is meant to be spoken with a hard 'G' and in this form it's a Hebrew name that means 'hill', so not quite the same romantic sense! But Mum stuck with her original spelling and pronunciation when she registered my birth in the UK. She had to repeat herself many times and spell out my name, to the amusement of the registrar. Thankfully, my middle name is fairly simple: Kate, after my dad's mum, who was known as Miss Kate on St Lucia. I use the name Kate when I am ordering takeaways or making restaurant bookings as I have found it less confusing for people taking the booking. Otherwise people mishear my name as 'Diva', 'Gina' etc. Mum is convinced that on the day I was born, back on 17 September 1984, it was foretold in the stars that I, Geva Kate, would eventually play goalkeeper, GK. There was no other position for me! I love her thinking and I love thinking that the stars maybe somehow did align and I have this spooky connection. Who knows? She and I are firm believers that everything happens for a reason. Sometimes you can't see the bigger picture but things happen and they happen for a good reason. And you always have to make the best of situations; you have to keep positive and believe that things will have a way of working out for the best in the end. I hadn't always thought like that but after going through some of the more frustrating and hurtful moments of my life, I definitely do. I've come out stronger as a person.

So, there you have it. I am often asked about my background and I say I was made in St Lucia and born in England. Apparently the midwife was shocked at how long I was when I was born. 'And she's still coming out!' she told Mum. I was 59 cm long so it probably was a bit of a shock! Rather annoyingly, my brother Raoul, who was born eight years later, was only 57 cm long when he was born. And now he is six foot eleven inches tall and I am only six foot two – but I do tease him that it doesn't matter how tall he gets, I know where he is ticklish and I will always be able to take him down!

Dad left the Caribbean and came over with Mum to England to be a proper family and when they set up home in Bournemouth, on the south coast of England, you could probably count the number of black people there on one hand. Did he come across any racism or prejudice? Most likely yes, not that he ever made a big deal out of it; his resilience was admirable. My mum's family took a while to accept the marriage. My granny was fine but my grandad took a little while to accept that his precious little girl had brought home a black man. He did come round and it wasn't a major problem; I think the attitudes of his generation were just different back then. Growing up, I never had an issue with race, with being the colour that I am. I never saw myself as something different. I don't recall ever being a victim of racism when I was growing up. I was completely fine at school even though at primary school I was one of only five kids who were black, mixed race or Asian. I never really saw my skin colour or my hair being different as a negative thing. I certainly didn't feel different. On reflection I think sport certainly gave me that respect from my peers: the fact was that I was one of the fastest runners at primary school; I could beat all the boys and people always wanted me on their team!

With Mum and Dad both being so sporty and athletic, it probably wouldn't have been too much of a shock that their children enjoyed being active too. I get most of my competitiveness from Mum but probably most of my athleticism from Dad. When they both came over to the UK to have me, he continued his sporting aspirations and played cricket, moving up to county level before getting into boxing and bodybuilding. It was always an interesting time when he was bodybuilding as he wasn't always in the best of moods before a competition. Bodybuilders have to fast to make their muscles pop out, it's crazy! And Dad would do an egg diet beforehand and get moody and snappy and you'd always know when he was like that and just be like, 'Oh, Dad's preparing for a competition.

Normal!' Although you'd know not to wind him up around that time – we'd know not to ask silly questions to annoy him!

Mum and Dad didn't want to be far from the ocean and we all lived in a house in Chessel Avenue in Bournemouth, which is literally a five-minute walk from the beach. Dad loves the water and I remember being very little and going down to the sea on his shoulders and staying there while he waded out. Some things haven't changed and when I am back in the UK we will still head down to the beach and go in the sea, whatever the weather and whatever the temperature. We will go in on Christmas Day, New Year's Day, whenever. It is the best feeling ever and I love it. You get a sense of your existence as soon as the cold water shocks your body but then you become accustomed to the sensation and you're treated to views of the beautiful coast-line, the Isle of Wight to your left and the Purbecks to the right.

I was an only child for eight years before Raoul, my brother, came along. Probably, for those first eight years, I was Dad's precious little girl. I say that because I remember one day, I must have been four or five years old, wandering out to where he was working in the garage. I spooked a stray cat that was sitting on the top shelf at the entrance of the garage and it jumped down in fright and scratched me. I still remember how cross and how distraught my dad was that this cat had 'scared his beautiful girl'!

We weren't ever allowed cats or any other pet growing

up; Mum liked dogs but Dad had grown up with the ideology that dogs were working animals and therefore never allowed in the house. So we never had one. Mum didn't like caged animals either, so we weren't allowed anything like gerbils or hamsters; the only pets we were allowed were fish. We got a couple of goldfish once and, although they were supposed to belong to my brother and me, I took ownership of them and thought of them as mine as I was the one who looked after them, fed them and cleaned the tank. Then one day I came home and noticed the tank was empty. 'Where's Bart? Where's Homer?' I asked, rather surprised and panicky. It turned out that my little brother had thought they were getting too hot and so decided to put them in the freezer. He was very careful, he said, he used the net and took them out very carefully. 'What do you mean they got hot?!' I fumed. Yeah, they were in the freezer. That was the end of Bart and Homer. As angry and upset I was at the time, I can look back now and see the good intentions of my then five-year-old brother!

I like the fact that there is a big age gap between me and Raoul; being the older sibling, I can remember a lot of what he got up to when he was younger – all the mischief – and I will have no qualms about sharing it all with, say, the guests at his wedding one day when I give a best woman speech! We are that close; he was a part of my entourage when I got married. He is my rock and from the moment he was born I felt such a protective bond with him. And that might have had something to do with the fact that I was there when he was born and I remember it well. Mum was happy for me to be there. I had been to her antenatal classes with her and we have such an open and honest relationship and always have done; nothing is a shock or taboo for me. She never hid anything from me or refused to talk about anything and I guess that is partly why I am so chilled now. I could have asked her anything and she would have answered me truthfully – whether it was about sex or where babies come from, alcohol, anything I heard at school or in passing. I could always go to her and she would answer truthfully. This relationship with my mum also allowed my parents to openly discuss with me how things weren't going well between them when I was five years old, although that trial separation didn't last long and only a few years later I was told I was getting a little brother!

On the day Raoul was born, I had no idea how exactly he was coming out, if that makes sense. Obviously I knew he was coming out of Mum but I had no concept of exactly how and I never made the connection between Mum's body and what my body might do one day. At the age of eight, I just watched what was happening, with no great under-standing other than that Mum was in pain and discomfort. We were in the hospital and Mum was lying on the bed and I was on the left side of her, Dad on the right side, up by her head. I remember they couldn't find Raoul's heartbeat and they stuck this massive pin-type thing up her, basically to pinprick his head to see if he had a heartbeat. Luckily, he did. Then the next thing I remember is him suddenly being there and lying on the table. Dad cut the umbilical cord and I was the first person to hold him. As I went to pick him up he peed on me and I know I thought that was disgusting! And then he did it again. 'Eurghh!' I said, as Dad celebrated the fact that 'it' worked! It's funny what little snippets you remember, isn't it? I know it was the middle of the day as well – I wasn't at school as it was the Easter holidays – and I know Dad's best friends were outside too. They were there to support him and I heard them giving him a bit of grief and joking with him. Little did I know at the time that one of the guys, Lawrence Dimham, would be asked to be Raoul's godfather and would end up living in Melbourne, Australia, not far from where I am based now! He and his family are all so incredibly supportive of me. It's brilliant to have them so close.

There wasn't any jealousy or worry that I would have to share Mum and Dad's attention with my new brother. I just felt pure excitement. In a way, I felt like a second mother to Raoul. My personality had pretty much formed, even at that young age, and I loved helping and nurturing him. I still love sharing and I love supporting people and I have always got most of my enjoyment and pleasure from looking after those around me. Even though I didn't realise it when I was young, I already liked to be with other people and have company rather than do things as an individual. I am quite comfortable in my own space and with my own company but I thrive on being part of a team.

My relationship with Raoul has gone from being like a second mother to him, to big sister, to friend, and now he is my rock. We support each other but he really is my champion. He totally gets me. He knows when I'm down, he knows what to say or what to do. He is at the heart of some of the decisions I've made in my netball career. I would pay more attention to the clubs who would offer to support and look after Raoul than those who would just offer me a good deal. Family was, and is, so important to me. My brother, my parents, my grandparents.

Mum had strong female role models when she was growing up. Her mum's mum, Evelyn, was a publican in Stepney, east London and her father's mother, Winifred, was landed gentry, but they were both suffragettes in the 1920s. So although my two great-grandmothers were at opposite ends of the social spectrum and their paths would never have crossed, both of them understood the importance of empowering women. Mum definitely had that instilled in her and it was natural for her to pass it on to me, too.

I was extremely close to my grandad, my mum's dad, growing up and when my grandma passed away when I was five years old, I became even more besotted with him. Dan Dan, I called him. I don't know why but the name stuck and the whole family ended up calling him that.

Dan Dan's real name was David Reeves and he was an

athlete himself, a 440-yard runner, as it was in those days (400 metres now). He was also a keen sailor and loved being on the water (a trait I have inherited), and I remember going down to the boatyard with him and him tinkering away on his boats. My love of sailing and boats developed from Dan Dan, although we didn't really go out on the water, we'd just get the boats ready for winter and he'd talk to me and tell me stories and then he'd take me home and make me bacon sarnies. It's funny what sticks around in your memory . . . I also remember that he would always give me a Werther's Original, which seemed like the best thing ever as I wasn't allowed those at any other time! He would spoil me rotten and I'd sit on his knee while he sang songs about an old lady riding to Banbury Cross.

As I got older we kept up our solid connection. When I walked home from school I would often call in to his house on my way. I am so pleased Dan Dan managed to see me play netball for England. He passed away over ten years ago but he saw me wear my England dress and he'd always ask me how I was getting on. He said he knew I would do well. If I tried my best, if I worked hard, it would all pay off. When he got very frail and ill towards the end I made sure I went to see him every day in his care home. It was so tough, seeing someone you love so much slip away and not be the person you want them still to be. He had given so much to me and taught me so much. I do miss him still.

Mum won't forgive England Netball for the fact that they neglected to present me with my first England cap, as she had arranged for Dan Dan to come to Wembley and watch me receive it. He was using a wheelchair then, very old and frail, and they had assured her I would be presented with it after this game. I should point out that this wasn't my first England game – for some reason I didn't receive my first England cap for a couple of years and it was something Mum had to keep chasing and chasing. I might let her tell you this story. I warn you, she pulls no punches!

'One thing that pisses me off is that Geva never received her first England cap. England Netball never gave it to her after she played her debut game. Yes, she gained it while away in New Zealand, but when I watched other players come and get theirs and the tremendous fuss that was made over them and Geva has only just received hers, eighteen years later! I spoke to them on so many occasions to ask them when they would present it to her and when they told me it was going to be awarded after a game at Wembley, I arranged for my dad, who was in a wheelchair, to come too. Getting to Wembley isn't easy, it's a long way from Bournemouth as well as travelling with a frail, elderly man, but I knew it would all be worth it. Dan Dan was so proud of Geva and it was going to be such a special moment. But they forgot. Nothing. No fanfare, no presentation – the game finished and that was it. My dad died a little time after that and so he never got to see his granddaughter presented with it. I will never forgive England Netball for that.'

* * *

Growing up surrounded by different sports was brilliant and I loved having access to them all. I wanted to try everything. I guess I was what you'd call naturally sporty. It wasn't that I wasn't academic as well, but doing sports, playing games, being active, that is what I loved. Mum signed me up to ballet lessons, then there was gymnastics, and then I found trampolining and that was that. Although before I started trampolining properly, I was asked to make up the numbers for the swimming team at my primary school, King's Park. The school was entered into a swimming gala and the teachers knew I was pretty sporty, so they asked if I wouldn't mind joining the team. We ended up doing so well and winning so many of the races that Mum was approached to see if I wanted to join the local competitive swimming club. They were impressed with what they saw when I swam, but she turned them down and I know that for a while she thought about how she never did discover if I could have been any good or not, and wondered if she'd made the right decision.

She told me a few years later the reason she had declined was because she couldn't bear the thought of getting up at 5 a.m., driving me to a pool, sitting by the side in the humidity and then driving home again. I remember telling her after she picked me up from a netball training session, that I had seen a group of cold, wet swimmers waiting around for their parents to pick them up and that they looked miserable and I would never want to do swimming. So I think that eased her guilty conscience a bit! It's true though, I am pleased I never went down that route. Being mixed race, having the hair that I have, I don't think it would have withstood that regular exposure to chlorine – my hair gets so dry! Swimming was just something I did a couple of times at primary school and I don't know whether I was amazingly good or just good for my age group. We won a few races but I couldn't tell you if that was me being especially talented or just that I didn't come up against lots of strong swimmers. Early mornings aren't a problem for me now but back when I was nine or ten years old, eurgh! I think Mum would have struggled to get me out of bed on those cold, dark winter mornings.

I come across a lot of swimmers now and I know what a gruelling training programme they have. Perhaps Mum knew it wasn't going to be right for me and she made the right decision. But that isn't to say I don't respect swimmers – or any athletes for that matter – who put their heart and soul into a sport. I get asked a lot in interviews who my 'idols' are and it's a bloody tricky question as, quite honestly, I admire so many people from all walks of life. Of course, the likes of Roger Federer, Serena Williams and Steph Curry are pretty high up, as are the athletes who I've watched still achieving their goals in their late thirties and forties and older, like Jo Pavey, Tom Brady and Kelly Holmes.

Before you think that my mum might be one of those 'pushy mums', making me do all these sports and trying all these things, she was – but only because I wanted to!

I never showed any interest in anything else. It wasn't like I wanted to go to the library all the time, otherwise she would have taken me. She did encourage me to try things other than sport on several occasions but they didn't work out. Music was one of them; she got me into the violin. I think I started playing the recorder at primary school (and yes, I think I can still play the start of 'When The Saints Go Marching In'), and then when I moved up to secondary school I saw all the kids turning up carrying these cool cello bags or violin cases and flute cases. I was like, 'I want to carry one of those!' Around that time there was a musician called Vanessa-Mae, who made playing the violin look so effortless and so cool as she played to really funky backing tracks. And I was like, 'That is me! I can do that!' So, I tried. I was desperate to get to the stage where you wiggle the strings really fast and your head and shoulders move in effortless rhythm. Do you know what I mean? I'm not exactly sounding like a top-class musician, am I?! Needless to say, I never made it to that stage. I was horrendous. Not just bad, really bad. I loved it, that was the thing, I really loved it and I don't think I was tone deaf, I just think perhaps I wasn't a natural. I probably needed to work harder on it or perhaps have picked it up earlier, before Vanessa-Mae made it look cool. Mum banned me from practising in the house, it was that bad. 'Worse than a group of cats all meowing,' she said, and made me play at the bottom of the garden. It probably got a bit too cold for me to carry on and I probably realised I was making a horrific noise rather than music and so I put the violin down. And never looked back. That's as far as my musical career goes! Trampolining, however, now that is another story . . .

2 A SWAN IN FLIGHT

'Those who don't jump will never fly.'

Leena Ahmad Alsmashat

SIGNING up to trampolining at ten years old was the start of my competitive career in that sport. I was a quick learner, I can't remember how many times a week I would train in the beginning but I think I was probably going to the sports hall three times a week. I would work with my first coach, Jane Chapman. She had coached two junior World Champions so she knew her stuff.

Raoul was only two or three years old at the time I started and while Mum and I were practising, he'd be toddling around getting into mischief. He was a right terror. The sports centre had a wide staircase and there was a nice water fountain feature right in the middle. It wasn't a wishing fountain per se but people had got into the habit of throwing their pennies into it and one time my trouble-some toddler brother went around scooping up all the coins. That wasn't the worst of it; another time he was caught standing at the side of the fountain, trying to pee into it! And then there was the time he pushed the fire alarm button and we all had to evacuate the building. It's a wonder we didn't get banned from the sports centre completely and that would have been the end of my trampolining career! I have so many memories from my trampolining days. I remember once I was going to my first music concert straight after training and I rushed to the changing rooms to get ready. I came out looking pretty cool, I thought, in my denim miniskirt and strappy vest top, but Mum wasn't impressed and made me change into something less revealing. I was not happy. I was on my way to see Peter Andre!

I was fearless from that first moment I climbed up on a trampoline and started jumping. I just went for it. To be the best, to reach the top level, you need to have this element and I think, especially when you are doing it for the first time, you just need to have no fear. Be 100 per cent into each bounce without holding back. Nowadays is a different story. I get on a trampoline and think, 'Ooh, this could go wrong if I try this move,' but back then, when I was younger, I was unafraid and that is something the coaches liked in me. I had been playing various different sports for a while by then, so I already knew how to hold myself, how to put my body in the right alignment. I loved being around the group of people there, the coaches and the other kids. It was so much fun. And the more I practised, the more I enjoyed it, and I started to learn some routines. Don't get me wrong, I wasn't rocking up each week just to bounce, learn some moves and then go home again. There has to be a purpose to what I am doing. I have to have a goal to reach, a point, as it were, to what I am doing, and so one thing led to another and I started entering competitions at weekends. I had a new coach now, Rosie Bascombe, and together with Mum we'd often travel around the country competing.

I had started secondary school by now and I was tall. I was five foot ten by the time I was twelve years old and I was still growing. My height wasn't ever something I worried about. My dad was tall, my brother was tall, so it was just normal to me. I wasn't ever teased about it, certainly. Even in primary school, where I guess I could have become self-conscious about it, because of all the sporty things I was doing my height always worked to my advantage. Especially in swimming, gymnastics and now trampolining. It was all about having the right body alignment, so I would always stand with my shoulders back and stand tall. You'd get better marks the better your posture and your extension – it shows strength. Why on earth would I try to hide my height? Standing tall is so important; how you carry your-self shows what inner strength you have. I see it so often with young girls now. They have that hunched-over look, they bend down, they are conscious of their height, and I'm like, you know what, shoulders back, stand tall, be proud of who you are and the height you are! Take confidence in your height. The only time I think I made an issue of my height was when I was about fifteen or sixteen years old and I had started playing netball properly. I had probably been six foot for about a year by then but I kept telling people I was 'five foot eleven inches'. It wasn't anything to do with shame or embarrassment, I think I'd just read that a lot of models were five foot eleven and it sounded so much cooler to be the same height as the supermodels. I was actually part of an Yves Saint Laurent campaign when I was younger. They were looking for tall, athletic, strong-looking women to be part of a 'Pink Amazon' theme and I went to London for the weekend, strutted around in six-inch plat-form heels, and then came home. Modelling definitely wasn't as cool as it sounded. I was going to stick to sport!

Mum reminded me recently of the time when I had started playing for England and I suddenly wasn't the tallest any more and so from that point on I made sure I got my height correct to the last inch! I was six foot two inches and proud. It gave me more of a presence. The taller you are, the more intimidating you are for the opposition. I think that is one of the reasons I found myself in a defen-sive position on a netball court; I liked the idea of being the last tall hurdle that attackers had to face. I was the last line of defence and so I wanted to stand tall and stand strong. I find it funny when I see the height some people have recorded themselves as, making themselves taller than they are. It happens a lot in netball and I'm like, really? You think you're that tall?!

So, back to the trampolines and one thing led to another and I started competing at weekends for a new club, Ringwood and Bournemouth, in various different competitions in our area. I was travelling around with Mum and Rosie and we would start moving further and further afield as the competitions and events came up. I was never able to control my nerves however. It became a big issue for me. Nowadays, I get nervous before a big game but I have found ways of dealing with it. I take myself away, I close my eyes, I nap . . . I allow myself to be distant until the moment I need to focus. Back then, in my trampolining days, I think my nerves became all-encompassing. I couldn't eat the day before a competition and I couldn't eat on the day either, so I would turn up to this big event running on empty. Then as soon as I had competed I would eat and everything would be back to normal again. I was trampolining for about five years in total and I just remember the nerves I used to feel; they still haunt me to this day.

When you compete in tramp first everyone performs the same set routine all at the same time, all on different trampolines. Then you do a routine that you have put together yourself. It's called a VOL – a voluntary routine. You have to add certain moves such as a twist, one move that has you landing on your front or your back and one move that has you doing more than one rotation. And you can put those moves in any order with seven other linking moves, so each VOL is ten moves in total. Then you are scored and if you rank in the top ten, you do your VOL routine again. That is when it gets the most intense. The whole arena goes quiet and it is just you performing, just your springs going, the whole place watching you. I just remember the sound the springs made as I was bouncing, knowing that all eyes were on me, everyone was looking. So many times I would crash out and land on the end decks or through the springs on the side. I couldn't handle it. I couldn't cope with the pressure of this individual sport; I was not cut out for it. When it's an individual sport, it affects you and you alone, and the nerves really did affect my performances. Your senses are so alert when you climb up on to a trampoline; you hear the murmurs of the people watching in the crowd, you hear every creak of the apparatus, every sound of the springs as you take your position, your heart beating, your own breathing, the sound of the springs. There is a panel of judges watching you – Are they whispering? What are they thinking? They are waiting for you to begin. You start counting yourself down into the routine in your head, then the moment comes and you rotate your arms to get them into the best position to commence your routine. You perform your first bounce and start your first manoeuvre but as soon as you are doing that you are aware of what has to come next; you have to prepare to move seamlessly into the next one, so you never really think about one move completely as you are always moving on, in your head, to the next one. There is such a heightened sense of sound, and yet everything is so eerily quiet at the same time. You need to try to think about your alignment, to not over-rotate each move, to keep your toes pointed, your arms extended and what move comes next, rather than worry about who is watching, what they are thinking or whispering.

And it isn't without its dangers either. I became a junior national champion and reached number four in the country at under-thirteen level, but I took some serious knocks along the way too. Getting back on the trampoline after a fall or injury is much like getting back on a bike or horse when you have fallen off. You have to keep going, you can't let that injury or that accident define you. But they do knock the confidence and I remember getting a corker of a black eye when I had just started secondary school – I think I was in year seven or eight – and feeling so embarrassed. I couldn't open my eye for a whole week; it was swollen shut and black and blue, and I looked like I had been in a fight. Not ideal when you've just started secondary school and have become more self-conscious. It was a silly accident as well.

I was at a training session in the sports hall and practising a new move. I was rehearsing a double somersault off my back and I came into the trampoline at the wrong angle and so my feet ricocheted back up to my knees, which in turn ricocheted back up to my face and I ended up fracturing my cheekbone. Luckily, the sports hall was just across the road from the Royal Bournemouth Hospital, so we just walked over the road to casualty. They didn't seem that surprised to see me there; it seems it was quite a common occurrence for trampolinists training over the road to end

31

up in A&E at some point! All the doctors and nurses were always so amazing when we went.

The odd minor injury coupled with the fact that I was still struggling to get over my nerves were probably a bit of an indicator for me. Mum said I looked like a swan in flight when I was up in the air but she also encouraged me to keep playing other sports during my trampolining years. Either she didn't want me to funnel all my energy into it or she knew that it probably wasn't going to be my defining sport. I suppose the final indicator, the realisation that my trampolining life was coming to an end, happened a year or two after my first accident. I was training at a different venue and I was working on another new move – a forward double somersault with a half twist. Anyway, I'm not sure if I blacked out or the sun blinded me through one of the skylights, but I ended up landing on the back of my neck on my trampoline before being flung onto another trampoline and then falling to the floor. It was pretty horrific, and I was put in a neck brace in A&E straight away. I had concussion and I was badly bruised and knocked but thankfully there was no permanent damage. Funnily enough, it didn't scare me or put me off trampolining – I probably would have climbed right back on the next day if I could – but Mum took control. I was still only just a teenager and I think the decision was, quite rightly, taken out of my hands. She sat me down and we had a conversation about what she thought. 'You are starting to grow taller and taller and it's harder to keep shapes and keep balance,' she said. 'You are growing out of your body a bit, Gee.'

Mum was just saying what I knew deep down – I wasn't cut out for this sport, not really. I used to crash out so many times as I had to bounce a lot higher than the others to get my limbs round each move, coupled with the fact that when I was competing I couldn't handle the pressure. So, with all this and together with the accident, I decided to call it a day. But I hadn't wasted my five years on the tramp. If anything, it helped shape the athlete I am today. It taught me some key ideas – about discipline, planning, preparation, timekeeping and work ethic – but it also taught me about myself as a sportsperson and the environment I work best in. This individual sport just wasn't the right place for me to succeed.

I did well in the odd competition but most of the time my nerves got the better of me. I was doing the odd bit of athletics too, the hurdles, during this time and whenever I used to compete, I was so nervous I couldn't eat all day. And now? Nerves are a funny thing. I suppose this was my first indicator that nerves are a real and common thing and part of the sport. But now I control them, they don't control me. I am part of a team now, so I have a bigger purpose than myself and that is my focus. I still get very nervous, don't get me wrong. I'll be in the England changing rooms and while some of the other girls are dancing around or singing, you'll often find me lying down, having a sleep or a doze. People might think I'm quite nonchalant and switched off but I am actually just lying there, listening to classical music, trying to chill out and not think too much. That is where my nerves still come into play; but as soon as I step onto that netball court and that whistle goes, they are gone. I am energised by them and I am in focus mode.

I guess sport helps us identify who we are as people as well. Are you an introvert? An extrovert? Do you prefer and thrive and perform better playing as part of a team? I know I do. I am not an individual sportsperson but I know athletes, swimmers for example, who do succeed by focusing on themselves and pushing themselves. It doesn't matter who you are, it's just about identifying it and using it to your advantage. So you might thrive in an office environment with a room full of co-workers, or you might prefer to be working by yourself. Or you might worry about letting a team down because, say, you have always had a psychological battle about being a weak link, and yet you are unstoppable when you work as an individual. Trampolining taught me that I wasn't an extrovert, I wasn't a confident bouncer who had an inbuilt belief in myself and my ability to perform as a soloist. I am a team player. And so I concentrated on the sport I spent most lunchtimes and breaktimes playing: basketball.

A lot of people see me now and they think 'basketball' rather than 'netball', because basketball is much more well known. I am trying to turn the tide on that way of thinking; it would be great for people to think 'netball' as they would of a world-famous sport – because it is! – but it's funny how people always assume basketball first. I did play basketball for a while before the netball court called. I had started playing a few years into my trampolining years, just at lunchtimes at my secondary school, and I loved every second. My secondary school, St Peter's Catholic school in Bournemouth, was a great school. I would rock up to the sports hall and join in with the boys playing basketball. It was, back then, more of a sport played by a collective mix from the school, some sporty types, some nerds and me, the only girl. Or, more accurately, me, the tall, mixed-race girl who could kick arse on the basketball court. I was in year seven when I first joined and I probably came across as more confident than I felt. To begin with I probably tried a bit too hard to fit in and impress them and they probably thought, 'Who the hell is this?!' They just wanted to have fun and relax at lunchtimes and then there was me, ultra-competitive! But as they got to know me and I got to know them, I relaxed and they realised I was actually all right. Then we would play the odd game and they realised I was pretty OK and invited me to join the team. I felt at home in a team situation, playing and working together as one side. I think I played on the team for the whole of year eight and playing against boys I would use my height to my full advantage. I would want to be intimidating and I definitely thought I was pretty cool. There was no girls' team at the school but I loved playing on the boys' team. And they were great fun and were happy for me to be on the team too. But other schools we came up against in matches weren't so happy. I was in year nine when I was told I couldn't play any more. Apparently word had got round that St Peter's had a girl on their team and the other schools started to complain. It was such a shame; we were unstoppable when we played, we beat most of the schools we came up against, and I am sure that is one of the reasons they complained – they didn't like being beaten by a school with a girl on their side! I am still really good friends with two of the guys I played with all those years ago. We became known as the Three Amigos: me, Laurent Rossi and Matt Ahan. They were brilliant basketball players and I love that we are all still in contact. We were probably a very unlikely trio back then; Laurent had bright red hair, Matt was highly intelligent, and then there was me, the six-foot gangly one. I didn't want to give up on basketball, even though playing for the school team wasn't an option any more, but I felt the sport had taught me about what I enjoyed most – being part of a side. Basketball is obviously a team sport but there are elements of it that are very individual. There are just one or two people who can win or lose a game for you and I would get nervous playing under this pressure. I would stress if it was down to me taking a free throw or taking a shot and would often pass it off to one of my team mates. 'What if I miss?' was becoming a thought that would enter my head frequently, and so, slowly, even this team sport started feeling more like an individual game. I realised jumping for the rebound and passing it on was my way of not losing it mentally on court. I was well on my way to finding my niche, to finding the right sport, but I wasn't there quite yet.

I still wanted to play basketball matches, though, so when I had to stop competing at school, Mum took me to a sports centre that she had seen was advertising for players for a well-established team in the area.

'This could be just what you need after trampolining,' she told me, and I agreed. And so we went into the sports centre. We didn't want to get in the way, so we stayed at the back. And we stood and watched. And waited. And waited some more. There was a training session happening, we understood that, but at no point did anyone approach us or signal for us to come forward. OK, we thought, they are obviously very focused in their training, we will wait until the end of the session. And at no point, in the hour we sat and waited, did anyone approach us or signal to acknowledge our presence. We were completely ignored. Mum was fed up by now and so when the session was over we went over to the coach to speak to them. Mum explained that I was interested in playing and joining the squad, how I had been playing matches at school, but they were not the slightest bit interested in having me on the team or in training. They did not give us the time of day. Now bear in mind, I was around thirteen or fourteen at the time, I was five foot eleven inches going on six foot, looking athletic and keen, and I didn't even get a chance to show them what I could do! At the very least you would think they might ask me to join in a session to see me play and give me a try. But no. And we just ended up turning round and walking out. It was pure rejection. Mum tried her best to lift my confidence as we walked out. She was furious. As a coach herself, she couldn't understand their lack of interest. And the strangest thing? We had watched them play a game and they were obviously short of players. It would have been an ideal time for the coach to get me to step in and see how I would fit in to the side. To this day I have no idea what happened. Mum probably took it to heart more than I did but she made sure I didn't feel rejected and so I knew it wasn't anything I had done wrong.

'It's all right, if they don't want you, there will be somewhere else that does,' she kept saying. However much she was fuming inside, she was so positive, she never let me believe it was my fault. Still it makes no sense to me, even now. If nothing else, it seems like a bit of a waste . . . I do a bit of coaching now and if I saw someone like that, someone like me back then, walk in to a training session, I'd say, 'Right, let's have you play here, let's see what you've got. No pressure, just give it a go.'

But everything happens for a reason. It was their loss and it was a turning point for me. I find it funny to think about how different my life could have been if I had been given a chance that day. With my height and skill, perhaps I could be playing professional basketball in America right now, instead of being based in Australia and playing netball.

I guess this was my fork in the road. I could have been sent on the path to the left but instead it was closed to me, which meant I turned right. I was on the correct path, I just didn't know it yet.

3 TAKING THE REINS

'No hour of life is wasted that is spent in the saddle.'
Winston Churchill

'**T**HERE is something we need to talk to you about, sit down.' Mum and Dad both looked very serious and for a fleeting moment I had to think hard . . . had I done something wrong? No, no, I don't think so. School was going OK, I was doing OK . . . I don't think this is about me. And I was right. It wasn't actually much of a surprise when they made it official that they were going to be splitting up. At fourteen years old, I wasn't stupid, I knew things weren't great between them. Raoul was probably too young to understand properly, but I was fine with it all. And that is all credit to Mum and Dad as they kept things very amicable. In all honesty, they probably get on better now than they did when they were married. Dad has now remarried and has two other daughters, which means Raoul and I have two half-sisters! I take my hat off to Mum – she had the foresight to see that at the end of the day, it is all about the children and some things don't go to plan but the children will end up being the grown-ups one day and what you instil in them now will help them when they are older. There was no animosity. We have had them stay over with us and we have spent Christmas with them in Holland where they live – Dad, his wife, his ex-wife and all his children. It's pretty incredible really, isn't it? It has taught me so much about relationships and life and how to look at the bigger picture. No one had died, everyone was OK. Dad was happy. He didn't shut us out of his life. The only thing that I think I was a little annoyed about was Dad never told us that he was going to get remarried. I think he thought we'd be too upset and so he just got married out in St Lucia and then told me and Raoul afterwards. He was nervous telling us, thinking we might be quite upset, but I told him, 'I'm the opposite, Dad, I would have loved to have been part of it!' So there you have it. The split wasn't a big thing and I saw them both and neither of them were upset at what had happened. Mum was always probably more influential in my younger years anyway and that hasn't changed. Dad would do shift work and do a lot of nights and we didn't really see a great deal of him during the week, so it wasn't really a massive adjustment.

I think the world of my dad and I have a huge amount of respect for him. I still see him when I can and I have a good relationship with him. He had quite an old-fashioned upbringing in that women were seen more as 'homemakers' but I think seeing Mum and me be so independent, successful and confident has softened him over the years. He has seen how hard I have worked to get where I am and he knows it hasn't been easy and he is proud of me. And I guess as we have got older, I have been the mediator between Mum and Dad – if they have any little disagreements I'm the one sorting it out, speaking to both of them. I love them both and I want them both to be happy, to continually respect each other and, most importantly, play a prominent part in my life.

It scares my dad how much like my mum I am. Before I moved to Australia I'd answer the phone when he called from Holland and he'd think it was Mum. We sound the same, although I do admit I have a slight Aussie twang now, but our sayings were and are the same and other than to look at us, you would never know! But I have got some traits from my dad too: I like to be more reserved in a group scenario, quiet almost, and will sit and assess a situation and not make any rash decisions, whereas my mum will be the talkative storyteller and never shies away from giving her opinion. Dad and I are both very cautious about our surroundings and sensitive to others, whereas Mum will drop people in it – she doesn't suffer fools and she doesn't hold back on her dislike for a lot of things. I guess what I am saying is, life isn't perfect. Things don't always work out the way you think or want them to. And I have the best relationship with my two sisters. I appreciate the small things a lot more with them around. I like just spending time with them, watching them grow up. Things aren't always going to be rosy but you have to make the most of it, ride out the tough times; and having that support crew around you who love you for you? That level of unconditional support is immeasurable.

Our house was never the kind that was empty and quiet. We had five bedrooms and Mum had decided to offer the spare rooms to foreign exchange students who needed somewhere to stay. There was a school just down the road, so it was ideal for them, and Mum was adamant that it was good for me and Raoul too. So we had an extended family.

Growing up in our big house with all sorts of different people was one of Mum's most fun and influential ideas. She was keen on us interacting with people from all over the world. She loved to travel, she loved to talk to anyone and everyone, and she liked to show off the area of Dorset we lived in. It was a real treat growing up meeting individuals from different backgrounds and different cultures, and we have kept in contact with some of them over the years and forged strong friendships; we've even spent Christmases with former students. They would stay in our home and be part of the family, eating breakfast and dinner with us and just being around. Mum wanted Raoul and me to be exposed to different characters from all walks of life; she was teaching us, from a young age, that differences are what define us and should be celebrated. Subconsciously, we learned not to judge people on where they came from, but just to accept them as the norm and get on with it. And hearing their stories about their travels and where they lived probably encouraged us to go out and see the world, to not be scared about visiting different places and learning new things.

Mum's love of travelling and her real sense of adventure have definitely stood me in good stead for all my travelling now with netball. When I was seven years old, I went to Iceland for three weeks by myself. Yep, all by myself! Mum put me on the plane and I travelled as an unaccompanied minor, with one of those necklaces that had all my tickets and passports and information attached. I had to carry that round my neck all the time. I don't know if you can even do that any more?! So I had no fear or worries about leaving home or being homesick; it was something I was used to from an early age. I was staying with a really good friend of Mum's who had a daughter the same age as me. I don't really remember much about that trip so I am guessing it didn't scar me for life travelling by myself so young.

I was quite independent and grown-up for my age and I was fearless when it came to horses. When Mum gets asked that question, 'What would Geva be if she wasn't a netballer?', she says I should have been a horse whisperer. I have a connection to them I can't explain. I was probably riding bareback when I was four or five years old. There is a photo of me riding alone on the beach in St Lucia. Dad had a couple of horses and would take me out for a ride, him holding the horse on a lead rein and me just riding bareback on the sand. That connection was always there, even as I got older. My godmother, Angi, had a 200-acre farm in the New Forest and Mum and I used to visit her a lot. Mum would sit and have a cuppa and chat for ages and I would go off and be with the horses. If ever they needed to find me I would be in the paddock, sitting on the horses, talking to the horses. I just loved that; it was just a nice way for me to get lost in my own thoughts, be at peace with nature. As soon as I started spending time with the horses, I felt calm. And I would relax.

When I was twelve years old I wanted my own horse but I was persuaded by Mum to have a pony on loan to begin with, and keep it at Angi's farm. The idea was that I would appreciate how much work went into having a horse – the expense, the time, the upkeep, the daily mucking out, the grooming, the regular riding. So I got loaned a twenty-five-year-old pony called Max from a lady called Mrs Cox. Mrs Cox said if I could handle old Max, who was blind in one eye and a bit of a character, I could handle any horse. Angi agreed to let me keep him in her stables and, to help me, she would put him out every morning and I would have to bring him in every night, groom and feed him and muck him out. Mum had to drive me there every day as the road was too unsafe for me to ride my bike, and it didn't take long to work out that this was never going to be a perma-nent arrangement. Going up there seven days a week took up a lot of time and both Mum and I realised having a horse was a nice idea but it wasn't very practical at this stage in my life. One Saturday morning we took Max out for a hack on a route that involved me riding him on a small country road for a short bit of the journey. Mum was walking next to me and Max when he suddenly bolted. Now I was a good rider but he was a strong-willed, stubborn old horse and he didn't want to stop! I tried turning him to his blind side but he kept on cantering sideways down the road and I just thought to myself, 'I've got to leap off, I just need to leap . . .' I tried to keep hold of the reins as I did so, but they ran through my hands and I was pulled forward, onto my tummy, and I let go. I could hear Mum shouting behind me and when she caught up, I think she was relieved to see I wasn't lying dead in a ditch! But I was in pieces: 'I've lost Max, he's gone, Mum!' I cried. I think her reply was something along the lines of, 'Sod Max! Are you OK?!' I was only twelve years old, so I suppose it was a bit terrifying for her. Max turned up back at the stables later that day looking very pleased with himself. But it didn't put me off horses and I kept helping and volunteering at Mrs Cox's stables.

One time I took out about five or six paying customers for an hour-long hack and I was on the lead horse (whose name was Commander, funnily enough), a beautiful pure-bred Arab, with the others following. We were on our way home and just before you got back to the stables there was a nice spot for a bit of a canter. So I signalled to the group that we would have a canter again, as we had done several times during the hack. We had just broken into a canter when a bird suddenly flew out of a bush and spooked all the horses. My horse went from a startled canter to a gallop and I struggled to slow him down. When I finally did, I turned round and saw that none of the other riders were on their horses! 'Oh crap,' I thought. 'Please don't have let anyone have broken any bones, I don't want to lose my job!' Not that I got paid for it, but I didn't want to be told I couldn't take people out any more. Thankfully, no one was injured. I collected all the horses from the cattle grid gate further down the route, where they'd all headed – horses are smart animals and they knew their way home – and got everyone mounted again, and everyone survived to tell the tale! I think they all enjoyed the excitement of that ride; they told me they had a great time. And yes, I was allowed to continue taking out people on hacks. These things do happen, you can't control a bird spooking a horse; it is about how you react and control the situation. I then spent the following two summer holidays in New Zealand with our cousins, who owned a ranch in Waitomo, on the North Island. I would work with the horses on the ranch, taking tourists who were staying at the nearby youth hostel for hacks across the terrain. There was no health and safety or English-style hacks of the kind where the group leader would ride out first and the others would follow in a line. We were just cantering and galloping over the beautiful terrain and it was utterly brilliant. And no one fell off that I can remember! It's not that I'm not allowed to ride horses now, but I do have to be careful as my sport is now my income and I can't afford to get injured before, during or after netball season. I guarantee one day I'll have some stables myself, with a few horses grazing happily.

Horses, and people from all walks of life, both played quite a big part in my childhood. The people who stayed with us didn't always progress to being friends for life though; we had so many different characters stay and some were just plain weird! There was a Greek guy, who was old and fat and hairy and who I once saw wearing nothing but these horrible white Y-fronts. I was leaving my room to head downstairs and caught him on the landing, coming from the bathroom back to his room. He was just sauntering around in his pants! I was mortified. I still have that unsightly image in my head to this day!

And I remember once we had a Spanish lad stay. He must have been about a year younger than me, fourteen or fifteen at the time, and he seemed very spoilt, always complaining. He was quite rude to Raoul and me on occasion. We got fed up of his attitude, so one day we decided to play a prank on him. One of the bedrooms at the front of the house has a window that overhangs the front door and when he came home from school we dropped a water balloon from the window all over him. It was summer, in our defence, and it wasn't like the water was ice cold, but he didn't see the funny side and cried. Mum was not happy and told us off, then explained that he had a lot of problems at home and we needed to understand his sometimes naughty behaviour was a result of frustration over his family life. 'Never judge a book by its cover' is a favourite saying of hers and I think I understood its significance for the first time then. And yes, it was probably a little mean, thinking about it now – but also it was only water! Toughen up! Raoul and I would always be spending time together and occasionally getting up to mischief, and I would forget that he is actually a fair bit younger than me. For example, I loved horror films (I still do). One evening I had invited some friends over and we watched *It*. I didn't notice Raoul, whose bedroom is next to mine, sneaking in to watch it too. He is to this day absolutely terrified of clowns. No joke – he is six foot eleven inches, a big muscly guy, and he's absolutely petrified of them. Whether it is a toy or a picture of one. I have scarred the poor boy for life!

I had a fun and adventurous childhood and things that might have had an effect on me growing up – my race or being tall – never did. I had differences all around me and was taught respect for everyone. I suppose sport has only intensified that ideology; people don't see my different hair or the colour of my skin, they see a person, my contribution to a team, my skill on court. I am judged by my ability. As an adult, I am probably more aware of my skin colour than when I was a child. I find myself more attuned to these things. I will go into a room and immediately be aware if I am the only person there with a tan. I am so conscious of it now that, if I am asked to be a guest speaker or if I'm just attending an event, I will look around the room and just scan and see if there is anyone of a different nationality or colour or appearance. I don't know why it is a thing for me now, but I think as an adult you are aware of what happens in the world, of the racism, the prejudice that can happen. People probably see me for me, they don't see me as mixed race or a braided-hair six-foot chick, and in netball there has never been any occasion on which I have felt threatened or intimidated by being mixed race.

I think the one and only time I was aware of any sort of racist comment was when I took my driving test for the first time. I was coming off the dual carriageway and I came off into the right-hand lane instead of the left-hand lane as I had someone coming up on the inside of me. My examiner said I had two minors and that major fail. 'In this country we drive on the left-hand side of the road,' he said. I didn't think anything of it at the time but I was upset about failing and I got in the car and told Mum what happened. She made me repeat what he said word for word and we ended up putting in an official complaint about him. I think we heard, about a month or so later, that there had been lots of complaints against him and he had his licence as a driving examiner revoked and had to go on a course to reapply for his job. But that is probably the only time I felt under attack for the colour of my skin. I am lucky, I guess, but I do feel I have escaped it because of sport too. People get behind you, they respect you for doing what you do. If you try a sport and you are not very good at it – whether it's running a 100-metre race or playing football or hitting a tennis ball – you have enormous respect for people who can do those things. When someone comes along and excels at something you know is tough, there is an appreciation, a respect, and you want to be around them. People don't see the colour of my skin, they see what I have achieved. Sport has given me the strength to be who I am and be respected among my peers.

So, you get the gist that sport was my thing. School-wise, I probably wasn't the most academic. Something has to give though, right? I loved St Peter's school. Mum was never big on making sure we got all the top marks; she always put more emphasis on us being healthy and happy and well-rounded kids. She never wanted us to follow a trend or do something just because everyone else was doing it. She made sure we knew the importance of standing up for ourselves and making sure we never judged anyone by what they looked like or where they came from. If you're brought up with these ideologies, you accept them quite naturally. And we did.

I was quite a social person and I had a lot of friends. I wasn't ever part of just a small clique; I could join any friendship group and get on with everyone, whether it was the arty lot or the music guys or the sporty lot.

I could move between different groups probably easier than others. I found it easy to mix with the boys – I wasn't a girly girl, let's put it that way, although I could quite happily hang out with girls. I was probably more of a tomboy. I found I could spend time with the boys and be more relaxed. I could just sit there with them and we wouldn't always have to make conversation or anything. I suppose I could just chill with them partly because of my interest in sport.

I didn't enjoy studying. I'm very practical and hands-on and I learn better that way than listening to someone talking to me or reading to me. I used to love geography, going away and doing projects and researching different countries. I loved languages, I found maths quite hard, and history was probably a subject that grew on me. And spelling? I wasn't great at that either – in fact, I would say I was atrocious . . . did I spell that right? So I probably wasn't the most academic but I did have a good work ethic. I tried!

A lot of what you learn and how you learn and how much you want to learn comes down to teachers. I had some great geography teachers and PE teachers who completely inspired me. I know what a difference a good teacher can make, so I am putting my money where my mouth is and I'm doing a Bachelor of Education Primary degree. I'm in my third year and trying to fit in all the study and practical sessions too. I've done a bit of coaching too; I've come across some pretty rubbish coaches and I thought to myself, how are these kids going to be inspired by you? There are ways of encouraging and making learning fun and that is what will help kids learn, at the end of the day.

PE was great at school too; the whole faculty was

awesome. Viv Hawkins was one of the PE teachers who helped me out when I started to play a bit of netball. She was always incredibly encouraging and I learned a lot from her. I guess this is where my journey as a goalkeeper really began, at secondary school, having finished trampolining and been snubbed at basketball. I think there were a few times I played netball at primary school but it wasn't like anything happened after that. Then, I think it was towards the end of year seven, or the beginning of year eight, my friend Caroline Marshall called me over to the netball court in the playground one breaktime. 'Can you join us, Geva? Just stand here and wave your arms and look scary . . .'

4 WHEN NETBALL FOUND ME

'The bird dares to break the shell, then the shell breaks open and the bird can fly openly. This is the simplest principle of success. You dream, you dare and you fly.'

Israelmore Ayivor

F basketball showed me how little it cared, netball welcomed me with open arms. There is no other way of describing it. Trampolining taught me that I needed to be part of a team, basketball taught me that I was close, close to finding the 'one', and on that gravel netball court one breaktime, I did indeed. Or netball found me.

I joined Caroline and my friends and every time they played, I played. It probably wasn't until the end of year eight, when I had played a few tournaments at school, that I started to get noticed. Two of the coaches at Bournemouth Juniors, a local club, had seen me play and asked if I wanted to join the team. Jacqui Berry, also known as the 'Godmother of Bournemouth Netball', and Pam Croft were both hugely encouraging when I joined, although I think the best thing about that was it was basically the same players we had in the school team so I was playing with my mates both at school and afterwards! There were a few extras from the other schools around too and we were pretty good, I thought. I was friends with Nina Quick, the goal attack from school, and Rachel Finan, a centre. Then there were girls who played for the club as a team but went to different schools, so when we played them in school tournaments we became almost enemies. That is how we saw it anyway. I would say 'rivals' but when you are young and take everything so seriously, 'enemies' sounds better! At school I always got picked to play first; I was a 'starter'. But when I played for the club, yes, I was tall but I wasn't the only tall girl there. There were three teams in the club, Bournemouth A, B and C, and for some reason I got moved to the older age group, up from C to B. It was around this time Mum spotted that Team Bath had a development programme in place that was run by Lyn Gunson, a former New Zealand Silver Ferns player. She was the coach and together with Waimarama Taumaunu, another New Zealander who had been newly appointed as England Netball's Performance Director, was on the lookout for future England stars. Mum, who hadn't had a clue about netball to begin with but was beginning to see there I had potential, was adamant I had to attend the open day at the university. I was only fourteen years old and she took me out of school to see what Bath University and Lyn Gunson had to offer. Can you imagine doing that now? Mum put so much emphasis on getting a good life balance – it wasn't all about good grades. I can't imagine my headteacher, Mr McCaffrey, being able to stop her even if he'd wanted to. Which he didn't, but more on my amazing school support a bit later. So while Mum had to sit through a lecture on nutrition and sports at the university, Lyn took me off to see what I could do on the court with a ball. I enjoyed the day and I think I made an impression but, most importantly, I knew this was what I wanted to do. I had found my sport, I had found my place, I knew I had to give it my absolute all. I was still playing for Bournemouth B team when I was invited to play for Dorset in an under-fourteens county tournament. It was in Gosport and the nature of these tournaments was that you went off in your little groups, said bye to the parents or whoever brought you, played for most of the morning, had a break for lunch, and then played again. You'd play probably ten-, twelve- or fifteen-minute games. Little did I know there were some England scouts who had come along to see what the south-west teams had to offer. It was at this tournament that two important things happened: firstly, Mum realised that I was actually quite good at this netball game and, secondly, I was T-IDed. Talent Identified. Spotted. Mum told me on the way home that she was sitting up in the back of the court watching the games and, whenever I played, some of the comments she could hear were, 'Who is this amazing goalkeeper?', 'Where has she come from?' 'What is her background?'

Mum, a short, white woman, was the perfect spy! No one knew she was related to me, the gangly mixed-race GK, and so she sat quite happily hearing wonderful things about me and feeling very smug. She could only be a spy for those early days though; now she is all over bloody social media and commenting on everything and I'm like, 'Mum! Enough!' She told one interviewer on TV years later that she gets so nervous watching me play matches she wets herself. I was mortified, I can't tell you the embarrassment. But she has also gone from being someone who never really liked netball as she never really experienced it at school ('Of all the sports, Geva!') to knowing all there is to know about the game. Considering she was so incredibly sporty, netball, she said, wasn't something she really 'got'. And now she is my absolute champion and gets so caught up in the games she wets herself!

At that match she was asked to give in my club details and the next thing I knew, I was invited to play in an opening ceremony for a brand-new sports complex that was opening in Bournemouth. It was called the Sir David English Sports Centre and I was put into the Dorset Seniors team, who were playing against some of the under-twenty-one England squad, by Liz Scott, a Bournemouth Sports Development Officer.

There were two netball courts at the centre and I can't tell you much about the match itself, other than I just remember feeling so incredibly nervous. There was a balcony where the crowd would look down and watch you and it was full of people. This was the first time I felt a little bit of pressure. There was expectation. Already people were asking why I had been brought in to play; was I good enough to be there? People were intrigued. I wasn't technically old enough for the senior side and I was set to be playing against some very decent players who were well on their way to making the England senior squad. I was fourteen years old and everyone seemed older and bigger and more experienced than me. And if England selectors were watching, what would they think? The worst thing about that match was the watching and waiting. The anticipation. I just wanted to get out on court to see what it was like, to see if I could keep up with the speed of the girls, whether I could get any intercepts or turn over any balls. I look back to those days and think how much my mindset has changed.

I started as goalkeeper and there is no other place on court I will ever want to play, but at the beginning it was all about me. I wanted to go out on that court and be the best I could be. Now I want to go on court and of course still be the best I can, but I am so focused on finding the right teammate to do that with. My goal defence. It is so crucial to be able to work together, to think what the other person is thinking, to shut down the attacking end. Now, it is about getting the best out of my goal defence and adapting my game to suit them so we become a strong defensive unit. I have played with some amazing GDs in my career: Billy Bowers at Team Bath, Sonia Mkoloma at Surrey Storm and England, Mo'onia Gerrard at Thunderbirds, Bianca

Chatfield at Vixens, Karla Pretorius at Lightning; but back then, I wasn't experienced enough in the game to appreciate how vital that was in a team, in a match. I was focused on myself, on making sure I shut down my player, making sure they didn't shoot. It was all about me. But that is youth and inexperience and pure rawness talking. I had come across from the individuality of trampolining and I was still learning the values of a team sport. One good player on the team isn't going to win you a game; you have to work together. So I sat and watched the first three quarters and then they brought me on in the final quarter. Dorset had lost the first three quarters and, as it turned out, had lost the match overall, but in that final quarter, the quarter I played in, we won. I am not saying I made all the difference, but I like to think I made a good impact and I was pleased that I made a difference to the team. I can't remember the actual score but I remember the mood afterwards. Everyone was so positive. One of the local newspapers was there, I think it was the *Bournemouth Echo*, and I was taken onto court for a photo. I had my weird hair back then; I used to have my fringe – well, two bits of hair that looked like antennae – that I would curl down and then I would keep all my frizzy, fuzzy hair tied back behind.

And hair idol or not, there were some pretty important England selectors watching that game and the next thing I knew I was sent a letter asking me along to try out for selection in the under-seventeen England team. The excitement was mixed in with a bit of naivety, I think: this was exciting but what did it mean? What would happen if I was chosen? Mum was probably thinking, 'Oh Jeez, where do I have to drive this girl to now?!' but for me, it was all about the next stage. Of course this was cool but what would I be doing at trials? What was next? Would I still be able to go horse-riding at the weekends?

It's pretty insane, looking back at it now. I was a fresh-faced fourteen-year-old who was fairly new to the game, and I was about to try out for the under-seventeen England netball team. The trials were up at Bath University one weekend and were split into two days. The first day was all about fitness testing, some ball skills and drills, and then the second day was all about match play.

One of the assistant coaches who is with us in the England camp now remembers me clearly from the first time she saw me at trials. Her name is Colette Thomson and she used to play for England herself. One of the fitness tests you had to do was throw a ball against a target on the wall for thirty seconds and see how many passes you could achieve. It was about quick, accurate, strong passes. Colette watched me as I came in and she said she was surprised that I had been put so close to the wall. Because I was so tall for my age, I should have been put at the five-metre mark, but because they had classified me due to my age, I was much closer. A lot of the testing I was smashing because of my height. And I had the strength and ability of some of the older girls but because I was younger, I had to be in the younger age group for testing. I was fourteen, in year nine, but looked and competed as if I was a lot older, which makes a difference.

It's hard to remember exactly how I felt about that weekend. I would have been nervous, like I was with most things, as I put such high expectations upon myself. Like in most new situations, I found it daunting meeting people I didn't know and being in new surroundings. Would people like me? Would I make friends? Most of the other girls knew each other from previous teams and I recognised a few familiar faces too. They were all nice and friendly. But in terms of nerves about what I was doing and what it meant – playing for England – I didn't have any. I love doing new things, I love challenging myself. Mum had signed me up for loads of things when I was younger and this was no different; I just had to go for it. It wasn't like I went that weekend thinking, 'I must get in the England team, my life will be over if I don't.' I approached it how I approach most things – by giving them my best shot and seeing what happens. Little did I know Mum had made friends with Eva Cookey, the mother of Pam Cookey who I was to play with in the England squad until she retired a few years ago. And there was another girl I met there too, Jade Clarke, who is still in the senior squad with me now and is the most-capped England player. But back then we were just three young girls hoping to impress selectors with our netball. Mum told me at lunchtime that she and Eva were chatting over a cuppa and how much they had in common. This process was new to both of them and they discussed how little they knew about netball and how neither of them had any previous interest or involvement in it. Mum was pleased she had found someone to pass the time with – it was a long weekend! – and they soon realised Pam and I were the two youngest girls there, with Pam just two weeks older than me.

After lunch things became quite brutal when the selection process kicked in. We were in the sports hall, with all the parents watching from the balcony, and suddenly we were split into two groups. Mum and Eva both said they initially thought we had been put in the 'thanks but no thanks' group and would be able to go home, but they were wrong. Our group was told we were wanted to stay and continue for the rest of the day and the other group were sent home. There were tears, girls grabbing their coats and storming out, some angry, most upset. That was the end of their trials. But Pam and I were still there. We were so excited but it felt wrong to make a big deal of it while the other girls were so distraught. 'I'm OK,' I thought to myself, 'I'm tired, but I'm OK, I'm still here!' So poor old Mum and Eva had to stay for another few hours with the other parents, while Pam and I went back for more training. Mum has often said to me that you can tell a lot about a player from their parents. Mum's mum and dad gave her free rein to pursue her tennis career and it paid off, but she played against so many kids whose parents, with no knowledge of the sport at all, would be on the edge of the court trying to coach or educate them. She saw so many kids dropping by the wayside because they got fed up of their parents trying to live their lives through them, and so I think from that moment Mum knew when to step up and when to step back. She told me that she had always believed in me and had the belief that, if I enjoyed what I was doing, she should just let me get on with it. As soon as that stops, you have to walk away. It seems so simple but watching some of the reactions from the parents of the girls who were rejected – they were angry and cross – you think, 'Hang on, who is more upset by the rejection?!'

It was a long day and by the end of it, when it was time to face the final cut, I don't think I was nervous about selection at all, I just remember being exhausted! From the sixty girls who started the weekend, forty had been sent home. Now it was just us, the final twenty, and we were going to see who would make the squad of twelve.

The protocol of how they announce a squad has varied greatly in my years for England. Sometimes you are given a letter, sometimes you get a phone call; it depended on the coaching team at the time and how they did things. This was my first experience of the process and, rather than be overwhelmed by it all, I just wanted to know one way or the other. We were all sitting cross-legged on the sports-hall floor, ready to hear our fate. Then in they came, the line of selectors, ready to deliver the news. 'We have seen such fantastic talent this weekend, well done everyone.' This was the start of the motivational speech. 'For those of you who have missed out, this isn't the end of the line,' and then they talked about girls who they wanted to put into a development programme and some they wanted to keep an eye on but who weren't quite ready yet. And then it was time to cut to the chase. 'We will call out the names of people in alphabetical order who have been selected. Please then come up and get your envelope. Congratulations.'

Pam and I sat there waiting and trying to work out if they had gone past our letter in the alphabet. Well, I did – Pam didn't have long to wait with the surname of Cookey. When she got her letter she stood over to the side with the other successful girls with a big grin on her face. I don't think I was concentrating on any name other than mine. I closed my eyes and willed myself to hear that familiar word . . . and then I did. 'Mentor,' they said and I leapt up to get my envelope. It was only then that I looked round to see who the other girls were, standing up next to me with their letters. We had all given it our all this weekend and had all gone through the same experience and now I would be seeing a lot more of my teammates! The letter you got was such a bog-standard letter – it was typed out and then after the word 'Dear' someone had handwritten the names. It was only when I opened the envelope and saw my name that the surreal nature of it sank in. I had made the England under-seventeen squad! Oh my gosh, I had made the England squad!! Mum says she was a little bemused by it all really but I remember that the car journey home, which took us an hour and forty minutes, whizzed by in what seemed like ten minutes because we were so excited! We couldn't stop talking about the weekend and the pure elation we both felt. Mum was delighted, I knew she was. She was so chuffed that – after trying gymnastics, swimming, trampolining, basketball – I could now settle into a sport I seemed destined to play.

Needless to say, when I got home there were lots of phone calls to make! All I wanted to do was sit down and rest and Mum was like, 'Geva, come and speak to Dan Dan,' or, 'Your godparents are on the phone, Geva, come and tell them the news.' Her levels of excitement far surpassed mine at that point, I was just so tired. And I had school the next day!

There wasn't time to sit back and reflect on what had happened that weekend. Everything seemed to move very quickly from the moment of being TalentIDed to playing my first game for the under-seventeen squad. Our first competition was called FENA and it was against Ireland, Scotland and Wales. We were playing in Manchester at the Velodrome, which was still being built for the 2002 Commonwealth Games. The day my England kit came through was the proudest day of my life! It was a second-hand kit from the senior squad but I was just so excited. I was only fourteen and had been playing netball for just over two years and I was representing my country – it was just all so nuts! I look at young girls now coming through the younger squads and rising through the ranks and I don't always pay them much attention or think too much about them. Then I have to remind myself that this was me once, that it meant so much to me then, that it meant so much to my family, just as it does now to the girls forging their own path through England Netball. Mum had arranged a photoshoot with me wearing my England kit, and still has the photo up in her living room. It is, unfortunately, hideous! But I was the proudest teenager you could imagine. The worst part of the kit was the red blazer, which had massive shoulder pads. I am posing on a chair, leaning on the back of it with my hands folded neatly in front and gazing off into the distance with a big smile on my face. It is so cringeworthy! But the fact it is still hanging up in my mum's living room shows how much it meant to the family.

The England under-seventeen experience is a bit of a blur. One of my teammates lived in Southampton and Mum would drive us both up to Manchester for training and matches. I remember one journey when we picked her up and she was buzzing with excitement. Mum and I assumed it was because she was going to represent her country at netball but she was so energised, she told us, because one of her good mates at school had just signed a record deal and she was so happy for him. We were impressed. 'Who is it?' we asked; her excitement was quite contagious. 'His name is Craig David,' she said. Ha!

I was on the team but I was probably third or even fourth goalkeeper in line. There was one girl who I would watch and just think she was amazing. They would call her Velcro fingers and she would just pull in intercepts from everywhere. 'I want to be brilliant just like you,' I thought to myself. 'I want to be able to rip balls in like you, I want to be that sort of defender.'

I did get my chance to show them what I could do too. I got the opportunity to play in every game. I was never a starter – this is when a team, at the beginning of the match, starts with their strong 'starting seven', their best players – but I played a quarter if not a half in every match. They were easy games at the time; Scotland, Wales and Ireland weren't as strong as they perhaps are now and we would win every match by about fifty or sixty goals if not more. Having that time on court meant that I definitely felt I had contributed to the team. I was part of something so cool. It's a spine-tingling moment when you stand on court and watch the England flag being unfolded and held up and then sing the national anthem. I know I have used the word 'surreal' before but it really was! This was just a normal weekend, I would be going back to school on Monday, and yet here I was now, singing 'God Save The Queen'! And that was pretty amazing.

I was fearless on court and yet, in assembly at school that following week, I was so embarrassed. The headteacher, Mr McCaffrey, announced that 'Our year nine sports star, Geva Mentor, represented the under-seventeen England Netball team at the weekend' and I had to walk up on stage as everybody clapped. Our assemblies were held in a theatre and I was so petrified of tripping down the stairs in front of the whole school, or walking up with my skirt tucked into my tights or something. That was fear. Not stepping onto a netball court at fourteen, against bigger, older, more experienced girls. Mr McCaffrey, apart from when he got cross when I came into school with braids and extensions in my hair a year later (something about it not being practical; Mum argued with him about how in Caribbean culture it was a way of taming Afro hair), was the most supportive headteacher I could have asked for. It wasn't like I was going around bragging about it; everyone at the school showed an interest, and so if anyone asked I would tell them. The level of support the school gave me really stepped up after that first tournament, when I started having to leave early two or three times a week for training. One of my PE teachers, David Dunne, who coached the rugby team, was especially encouraging.

You'll have to excuse me if the following account goes past in a bit of a blur, as it certainly did for me. The FENA games were early in 1999, around February time. I didn't realise but at those games was the England Senior Coach at the time, Julie Hoornweg. Lyn Gunson, her assistant who had seen me briefly in Bath, agreed that age shouldn't matter and, knowing I was 'one to watch', sent Waimarama Taumaunu to come and watch me play in a county match. I was playing for Dorset County and the match was against Surrey County but we were only the warm-up game as, after we played, the England under-twenty-one side were scheduled to play the under-twenty-one Jamaica side. Waimarama Taumaunu came early to watch our match and liked what she saw. I was shaking up the game; I was young and fearless and making a big impression against girls who were a lot older. I believe my naivety actually stood me in good stead as well – I didn't overthink things, I just played. Liz Broomfield had got my mum and my PE teacher, Viv Hawkins, tickets to that game and she went over to Mum afterwards. 'Geva is going places,' she said, and both Mum and Viv told me afterwards how they were bursting with pride. It was after this that I was invited to come and train with the under-twenty-one England squad, who were taking part in the World Youth Cup the following year. So we went up to Cardiff and met with the squad, who were all a lot bigger and a lot older than me, and I felt totally out of my depth. But I knew I had been asked to train with the side for a reason and so I just went for it. I met one of my best goal defence partners there, Sonia Mkoloma, who was also to become my best friend off court and would be maid of honour at my wedding years later.

Now, prior to me, fresh-faced and having only recently turned fifteen, training with the under-twenty-ones, England Netball had quite a rigid training and playing set of rules. If you were under seventeen, you played under-seventeen, if you were under twenty-one, you played for the under-twenty-ones. If you were over twenty-one and considered good enough, you went into the senior squad. That is how it worked until Julie, an Australian with her own set of ideas, together with the performance team of Lyn Gunson and Waimarama Taumaunu, changed the

England set-up. They didn't believe age should be a barrier. If you were good enough to play in the senior side, whether you were ten years old or forty years old, you were in the team. And so it was that, after that very brief training session with the under-twenty-ones, Mum got a phone call on Wednesday morning inviting me to come to Loughborough and trial for the England senior squad.

I remember Mum being in such an excited panic as we had to make a quick decision. Was I happy to drop everything, leave school that afternoon, and travel up to Loughborough with Raoul in tow? My reaction? Of course I had to do it; there was no question. And so Mum drove us all up.

Try-outs for the England senior squad were very much like the under-seventeen selection process. They were conducted over two days, with the first day devoted to fitness testing and the second day all about match play. We went into the Sir David Wallace Sports Hall at Loughborough University on that second day to play our games and there was a balcony filled with all the selectors, the coaches, members of the England staff looking down to watch. And instead of being nervous, I felt completely at home. I had no worries in the world. I think Mum's words were ringing through my head – when we were driving up to Loughborough she told me something that her coach had told her when she was playing county squash: you fight for everything, you run down absolutely everything from the off and you stay like that until the dying seconds. You get inside your opponent's head and in those final moments of a game, when they are starting to crumble from having you constantly chipping away at them, you win the game. It isn't just about winning a quarter, it's fighting until the last second and not letting up on your opponent for a single second.

When it came to that match-play day, I played fearlessly and committed to everything. I was young, I was happy to run out of the circle and do flying intercepts and if that meant I would knock someone down accidentally I did, although more because I was Bambi-esque and didn't have full control of my limbs. Obviously I would pull the other player back up again! But I played like I had no fear. I think the selectors must have liked what they saw – this young goalkeeper wasn't afraid of stepping away from the post and coming out of the circle, which wasn't the norm at the time. I let my play do the talking and at those trials in October 1999 they selected me, fifteen-year-old Geva, to form part of their England senior squad. In the space of a year I had gone from getting a place in the under-seventeen squad to playing in an international tournament, to training with the under-twenty-one squad, then getting invited for selection with the England senior team, and finally to being offered a place not just within the England squad but as part of their team of twelve. It had been one hell of a year!

5 EARNING MY STRIPES

'Patience is not simply the ability to wait – it's how we behave while we're waiting.'   Joyce Meyer

I F 1999 was a whirlwind of excitement on court, 2000 was going to be a year of watching and learning from the sidelines.

I had been picked for the England seniors and there was a test series in England against Australia that was going to be my first taste of international netball at a senior level with the squad. Australia were the team to beat back then; we knew they would beat us easily, by thirty or forty goals, but the test series was important as you don't improve unless you play against the best. I was so excited just to be part of the squad for those test matches that I don't think I minded that I didn't actually play. The whole experience was about exposure and learning and I'm certainly someone who gains a lot from sometimes sitting back and watching at first.

For all of those three test matches against Australia, being played in England, I sat on the bench and I think I was OK with that. I say that – obviously I would have wanted to get out there and play; I was eager and young and I might not have fully understood what being part of a squad meant back then. It was a rite of passage. You don't just come into the squad and get a game, you have to show you are part of the team. I'm a firm believer now that it isn't just about exposing people to court time, it is letting them earn their position. And that doesn't always come easily. You have to challenge those on the court who are playing in your position and you have to fight to get on; it's what I've come to know is healthy competition. You can't just be handed your caps. It is a valuable lesson you learn that you have to ride the bench, you have to keep it warm, so to speak, and that is an important part of being a netballer and being part of a team. My thoughts were along the lines of, 'I can still make sure I am giving feedback or coaching points to the girls as they come off. I can still tell them what I can see, what is happening on court to improve their game and improve the team performance.' Finding the confidence to give helpful advice to my peers, who were all senior to me, was definitely a daunting experience but an important lesson; if I was confident in what I was saying I shouldn't feel self-conscious.

Sitting on that bench builds character: you learn to contribute, you learn from those around you, you learn to encourage and interact and bide your time. I was OK to be on the bench as I was ecstatic to be in the senior squad. I appreciated what the players were doing, and if they were better than me then they should be the ones on court. We were a team. Of course, Mum wasn't quite so understanding at the time. Her little girl had made the England team and she didn't understand why I wasn't getting a game!

Every test match that series she had brought different members of the family to travel up and watch me play. At the first match she had everyone hold up a piece of paper that would spell out my name, but they were never able to hold them up as I stayed on the bench the whole time. In the second test she came with her friend Pat Mathie and her daughter, Leanne, and things looked promising in the third quarter when the GD, Amanda Newton, was injured and they thought that would be it – I'd be on. But no. In the third test Mum came with six of her cousins and they ended up sitting next to Jill Neville, Tracey Neville's mum. Tracey was playing at the time but, of course, I stayed on the bench in that final match too.

Mum decided to ask Lyn Gunson after that third match why Julie wouldn't bring me on for the last quarter, especially as we were being so badly beaten that it wasn't like it would have mattered to the overall result. And Lyn's answer was simple. It was easy to make the squad of twelve, the difficult part was getting on court. And when you do, you need to make sure you are a starting contender. She also told Mum that the Australian side we were playing were a rough, tough, take-no-prisoners side and she wanted me to experience that game from courtside. She was also watching how I reacted to the game and what motivation I brought to the other players. She knew it was important, Mum now understood its importance, and I definitely feel it taught me something – I was still a vital part of the squad, even if I wasn't on court with the team.

I learned some big lessons that first year, about staying focused and staying positive and knowing that my time would come. It's an important thing to remember when you aren't playing, either through deselection or injury; you just have to bide your time. You're always going to have moments in life where you don't think you are where you should be but you have to have patience. This is something netball has taught me and I guess it applies to any work environment. You didn't get the promotion or someone else got picked for a work project over you, or you feel like you are just going through the motions without ever getting notice. Patience, resilience. Keep doing what you are doing – which you are doing perfectly well – and the opportunities will come. I see so many girls coming through the England set-up, gunning for court time and despondent when they aren't picked, without seeing the advantages of spending time on the bench and learning how to read the game. It's all about self-belief.

* * *

In September 2000 I turned sixteen. 'Forget the piercings, everyone is getting a piercing, G, be a bit different!' Mum was right. I wasn't that fussed about getting more than one hole in my ears but I did want to do something to mark turning sixteen and to commemorate the fact that I was part of the England squad. But what?

And then she came back from the dentist with an idea. Pete Gilfedder, who is also a close family friend as well as a great dentist, had showed her a tooth jewel, a new idea from Scandinavia that required the dentist to glue a sparkly jewel on to a tooth. Mum was convinced that these 'twinkles' were so individual, unique and cool that they summed me up perfectly! Plus she was told they weren't meant to last long so, in Mum's eyes, a perfect solution! I chose a dolphin as I think they are amazing creatures – they seem so free and graceful – plus I've always had an infatuation with the sea, probably from living so close to it. It made sense. Mum was right, it was a nice treat to celebrate a brilliant year. My first one lasted a couple of years, although they are only meant to last a year or so; I lost it after it came out when I bit into an apple. The second one lasted a bit longer but I don't know where that went; I think I might have swallowed it, so we all know where that ended up! And the one I have now has lasted for yonks and I forget that it is even there. People who I have known for ages don't always spot it. Even the other day, a girl who I've been playing against for years was like, 'Oh gosh, I never knew you had a dolphin on your tooth!' My brother thought it was so cool he went and got a scorpion. I quite like the fact that we both have one. It's like our little shared sibling sparkle.

The following year, I was selected again to join the England senior squad as they embarked on a tour of New Zealand and Australia. It was a seven-week tour and I was in the middle of revising for my GCSEs. The school were brilliant; I was to take lots of revision material out with me so I had plenty to work with. Travelling to another country with eleven other girls to represent the country at netball was a pretty unique experience. I wasn't homesick as I had been away before when I was much younger, but I was still relatively young and so I did appreciate having our amazing welfare lady, Margaret Palmer, with us. She was like a second mum to me and took me under her wing and having her there was a comfort; I could concentrate on netball and not be missing Mum and Raoul too much. I knew that this might be the series I would get some court time and I was preparing myself for that. We played a couple of games in Australia to begin with and then moved to New Zealand, where we would be facing the formidable Silver Ferns team. I remained on the bench in that first match but I was conditioned to the idea that this was good for me, this was OK, I was still part of everything that was going on. I had started to read the games really well and made sure that I gave constructive feedback to girls as they came on and off. We moved to a venue in the city of Palmerston North for the second match and things started off the same as any other match day. We would do what is called a 'captain's run' in the morning, when the captain would take us through a warm-up and a few drills. It was our opportunity to familiarise ourselves with the court and the arena as a whole. We wouldn't be back until the evening for the game, so it was important to see and experience the surroundings first. When I say arena, that's a bit misleading – it was like a big farmyard shed or an aeroplane hangar. It was no big fancy venue, it was cold, and there were fold-up chairs round the side and a makeshift court right in the middle. But this was New Zealand and they loved their netball and so we all knew the crowd would be bloody vocal! At the start of the captain's run we got into a huddle and we all put our hands in the middle. Something didn't feel right to me. 'Where's Chioma?' I said, looking round. She was one of the girls on the team and she wasn't here . . . we had basically hopped on the two buses that morning without checking we were all on board! We had to get someone to call the hotel and go back and collect Chioma and bring her to the court. I remember it well, it was quite funny in the end but, for a split second, a bit of a panic! The main reason I remember details like this from that day was that this was to be my first match; I would get my first cap for England on that day, 11 July 2001. I can't remember exactly how the announcement for the starting seven was done that day. This lack of specifics probably reflects the way I am: I just take things in my stride as they happen. It varies from game to game and from coach to coach. You sometimes get told the night before, sometimes it is in the morning on the day of the match, and sometimes it is when you are in the changing rooms an hour or so before you are about to go on court. I can't remember, that first time, when exactly I was told I would be part of the starting seven. But what I can remember from my first cap was the line-up before the game, standing there, arm in arm, singing the national anthem with my teammates. Before we started to sing, there was lots of whispering from the line: 'Look!' came the whisper, 'the All Blacks!' and we all turned to see the New Zealand rugby team coming in to watch. Apparently one of the players was dating one of the Silver Ferns players, Anna Rowberry, and so the whole team had come to watch the game. It was very surreal as they are like rock stars in New Zealand! Then the national anthem kicked in and we all got serious. After singing you head to your position on court ready for the umpire's whistle, but just before that, in this sport, the first thing you do is greet your opposition player. This is the person who, for the next fifteen minutes, you will be trying your utmost to upset and disrupt. Some players do a quick high-five or a handshake. But I knew who I was up against, a legend in netball, and back then one of the most capped international players of all time: Irene van Dyk. Irene was born in South Africa and moved to New Zealand in 2000, the year I was earning my stripes. She was a dominant force for the Silver Ferns for many years and is regarded as one of the best goal shooters in the world. Even though she was such an icon I wasn't intimidated or frightened about coming up against her. When I went over to greet her she just put out her arms and pulled me in for a giant hug. Then she kissed me on the cheek. Well, I wasn't expecting that! And then all of a sudden the whistle went and the ball got thrown into the circle and I came across with an outside hand and managed to get a tip, my outside mid-courter collected it and we went down the other end. Then it was our centre pass, then it was their centre pass, and then the ball came down our end and I ran out and got a deflection, which I gathered to intercept, just outside the circle. And then the ball went down our end and I don't think we scored – I remember in those England days, our goals percentage was a lot lower as we struggled to convert most times – and then the ball came back down to us defenders again.

I can't remember if I stayed on for the whole thing but I remember those first couple of minutes of the first match I ever played for the England senior squad, nearly twenty years ago. I was playing elite international netball against one of the best players in the world and I did my job. I am a goalkeeper, I am the last line of defence, my job is to disrupt the opposition's attack end and I did just that. I got my hands to the ball, I turned it over for the team. I think we went on to lose by about thirty-six goals but it wasn't quite one of the forty-goals losses that we had had before. And the next game, they started with me again and we only lost by twenty-two goals . . . I know it is still a loss but you've got to find the positives – the margin was decreasing! I gained my first cap in rural New Zealand against the world number-one shooter, against the Silver Ferns team, who were number two in the world and, I have to say, it was pretty cool.

I had the realisation that I was properly part of the team now. There was no official cap, medal or certificate, just a card from my team and some flowers, but that was special as it confirmed all the training, all the time I had spent on the sidelines, and now I really felt I was part of the twelve-woman squad. It was an incredible feeling for a sixteen-year-old!

Unfortunately, until you get on court and experience that first taste of elite netball, you don't truly feel like you are contributing and what part you play in the team. No matter how inclusive your teammates are, it is very difficult in netball as there are the seven or eight who are always on court and then there are the four or five girls who are always on the bench. Those of you on the bench start to form a sort of 'clique' – no, that's the wrong word . . . you form a bond. You form a bond because you go through an exhilarating adrenaline-filled experience for anything from fifteen to sixty minutes. It is difficult not playing. I've been there, I know. While everyone who has just come off court does their cool-downs, you have to go on and do drills, shuttles, all sorts of training as everyone is exiting the stadium. You have to push yourself to fatigue to keep the training load the same as the ones who have played. It almost feels like a punishment. It's obviously not but it's the last thing you want to do as, although you weren't physically out there, you've just gone through the emotions of the game and it feels like you were playing and you're exhausted. So as much as being on the bench is part of the learning, it is difficult. I knew and appreciated what it was like for the girls on the bench who don't necessarily get on to court and I know how important it is to make sure they still feel part of the team. It's funny how for me, after my match with Irene, I felt: 'Yes, I am contributing to this team now.' Contributing in a way I thought I was better at, through playing, not coaching.

I had ticked all the other boxes and this was the final one: I was on court and playing, which at the end of the day was what we were here to do. The buzz the next day, after my first match, was amazing. We went to Queenstown, if I remember rightly, and the scenery was just breathtaking. They love their netball in New Zealand and the local paper wanted to do a story on me. Apparently the youngest netballer playing for her country was news! I say this because netball didn't have any real profile in the UK at the time. A photographer came out and took some pictures of me while the rest of the girls were getting ready inside for a court session. We went outside and I had a backdrop of the Remarkables, a beautiful mountain range. And the photographer set me up for some leaping shots, so there I am jumping, posing, being photographed in this stunning country for a newspaper that wants to tell everyone how I played on court. I had never experienced any sort of media interest before then and, I have to say, it was pretty cool! And then the next day or the day after there was an article in the paper and a really nice photo. I bought a few copies and I sent the article to Mum as I knew how much she wanted to have been there for my first game. But not only were the flights expensive, it was a long tour and Raoul was still in school. We talked a lot on the phone so that was cool, and although it was sad not to have Mum and Raoul there I was able to fill them in on everything that happened. And on how I was probably just as excited that the All Blacks came to watch our game as I was at getting my first cap! I still have the photos and the article from the paper too; I have kept it in a scrapbook. I've also kept a 'cap' book, a record of all the games I have played for England. I record the date, where we played, the score, the starting seven and the girls in the team. I am the only one keeping a record, I think, but when I retire and get presented with a nice red, leather-bound cap book, I will get someone to write up all the details beautifully.

Travelling with eleven other girls meant that you didn't ever get the chance to really feel homesick or lonely. There was always someone to chat to or do something with. It was a bit like having a netball family. All of the girls wanted to make the most of visiting New Zealand, so they would plan sightseeing excursions around our training and matches to make the most of being over here. This, however, did not apply to me. I had to study for my GCSEs, so while the others went off for their fun adventures I was a good girl and took myself off to the physio room, where a little desk had been set up for me to revise. Glamorous, eh?! But it was one of the stipulations of me being allowed to join the team on tour – I wasn't allowed not to complete my GCSEs. And I did have special dispensation for some of the exams. I didn't have to sit many; for a lot of my subjects, grades were taken from previous assignments and classwork. I think I only took two or three exams in the end. I did OK in them – well, maths wasn't great but the rest of the subjects were Cs or above with an A* for PE. And you'd bloody well think so considering my involvement in and understanding of sport! All in all my GCSE results were not bad for someone trying to train, play at the elite level, study and still be a teenager all at the same time!

I didn't just come back home with my first England match experience under my belt, I somehow managed to come home with a fridge-freezer too! Every time we went to play for New Zealand – and I gathered this right from the first tour – their hospitality was pretty awesome. After every game, you have your recovery session and then normally have a dinner. I remember going up to a conference room after the final game. It was a chance for both teams to chat and then the captains would do their speeches. This time they had arranged for a fun game to be played and they wanted everyone to join in. They had set up this big washing machine, a top-loading one, in the room and the competition was that you had to 'shoot' a netball into it. Every time you got a ball in you would go through to the next round and it was only a bit of fun but everyone got into the spirit of things. So it was England versus New Zealand again and this time there was no one on the bench – the team physios, the coaches, the doctors, everyone tried to launch the ball into the washing machine. Now, I am not sure if I've mentioned this but there is a good reason I am goalkeeper and not goal shooter. I'm the twelfth shooter in line on the team and, honestly, I am OK with that. I knew from the moment I started playing netball that I was a defender. I haven't ever wanted to play in any other position other than defence; it is where I am, it is who I am. Each person on the team fits into their role and I have always had a defensive mindset. I started off as goal defence at school because that's kind of where I just got put. When I moved up divisions and played for better teams and better opposition they moved me back to goal-keeper as I was quite tall and I was able to handle the taller shooters.

You sometimes come across defenders who have been given a go at shooting by their coach – Ama Agbeze is a classic example; she was a goal defence, moved to a shooter and then back to defender – but I am pleased to say that has never happened to me. I am quite happy where I am. I have played some training games where you rotate through the positions but I bottle it when it comes to shooting. You see, everyone on the team has different personality traits, which is why they fit into their positions. What you are like on court is very much a reflection of how you are in life. Defenders? You tend to find us quite laid-back, quite chilled. We won't take life too seriously, we like to have a bit of fun. Midis – the mid-court players – they are the engines of the team. They will go, go and go again. They are the real workhorses of the side, and they are often the bubbly, big personalities of the team. And then you have the shooters, who tend to be known as the princesses of the team. If the ball doesn't feel right to them they'll want to change it. If the ball doesn't feel right to us we're just like, 'Oh well, who cares, let's get on with it!'

Shooters can be very high-maintenance and like everything to be a certain way. But I won't knock that trait as when the pressure is on they're the ones who have to put the ball in the ring. I guess you have to be a bit like that because it sometimes comes down to the finest detail about whether you are going to make that shot or not – how the ball comes off your fingers, how your body positioning is, what happens around you. You have to have that attention to detail as a shooter, you have to have that picky mentality. They are also a bit cocky and a bit arrogant but they are playing in an under-pressure position – all eyes are on them, the crowd are on the edge of their seats, they have just one final shot of the game to win a match . . . so of course they need that self-belief that they are going to make the shot. They really do have nerves of steel but, in essence, they're definitely a different breed to the rest of us – says every defender!

So, back to how terrible I am at shooting. I expect the majority of the people in that room thought that Irene van Dyk would be the one heading home with a new fridge-freezer, so no one was taking it too seriously. Everyone seemed to be doing a netball-type shot into the washing machine so I went for the underarm, between-your-legs type lob instead. And it went in! I was chuffed not to be out first time and so waiting for another go. There were still a handful of people on each side and I went round again and I got it in again! Then it was only me and a New Zealand physio left in the competition. She lined up like before, the washing machine a good five metres away. She took her shot and missed and I took my shot and got it in. Just like that, I had won! It was completely surreal and no one in the room, including me, would have ever predicted it.

I rang Mum afterwards and was like, 'Mum! I've just won a fridge-freezer!', to which her reaction was something like, 'Where's that going to go then, Geva?' She didn't get the excitement at all at the time, but it is still in her house, this big stainless steel Fisher & Paykel fridge-freezer, on the upstairs landing, and I know she has found it useful for all the students to use. I got asked after I had won it whether I wanted the doors to open to the left or to the right and I was like, 'Erm, I'm sixteen years old, I have no bloody idea!'

It was quite cool to think that all this was happening while I was still at school. My GCSEs done, I was now studying for A levels – and playing for England. As well as my headteacher giving me the best support at school, my PE teacher, Patrick Lucas, was the most encouraging person I have ever met. He was an ex-London Irish rugby player who had had to stop playing for them in the nineties after a serious injury. We just hit it off straight away. He had motivated me quite early on and helped me follow the training schedule that England Netball had put together for me. It was quite an intense programme and he didn't let me just 'tick off' each section, he really made sure I did it with extra intensity, extra passion, extra quality. He also made up some drills for me; he wanted to push me to see the benefits of training hard and training well. I learned a lot from him and he understood me too. He had a real understanding of what it meant to play at an elite level. He gave me the advice that he had been given when he was playing rugby, which was always to look out for myself. 'No one is going to look after your body but you,' he said, 'you are literally just a plate of meat and you need to make sure you look after yourself because if you get injured, don't think there won't be ten other girls ready to step in and take your place.' It was sound advice that I probably didn't appreciate at the time but as I get older I certainly do. I helped him one summer with a rugby clinic he ran, and worked with the rugby schoolboys on ball-handling, as rugby and netball have lots of transferable skills when it comes to handling and spatial awareness. He knew that playing these rugby games would only improve my skills on the netball court.

But even though I was benefiting from having such a dedicated trainer, I decided at Christmas that I needed to put myself in the best possible position of being selected for the England team for the Commonwealth Games the following year. They were being held in Manchester and although I had a good chance of being in the squad, it was never a forgone conclusion. I had to show how serious I was about being part of the team and that meant joining the training sessions with England coach Lyn Gunson in Bath. And so I did just that: Mum would drive me up to Bath twice or even three times a week. Raoul would join us on occasion and we'd just sit back and play silly games while Mum spent the best part of her week driving. She would never complain about it either and I didn't appreciate how tiring driving could be until I learned to drive and made that journey myself a bit later.

The training sessions were quite nerve-wracking, if I am totally honest. I was nervous, never sure of what they would involve. My skill level wasn't as polished as it is now and I was so focused on trying to do my best, not drop balls, not be the weak link. I was training with girls who all had a bit of experience behind them but they were all nice and encouraging to me. There was a school we used to train at, Monkton Coombe, which was really dark and dingy. The sessions were tough – I am happy to admit I found them quite intense – but it was fun. I used to treat myself to something from the vending machines afterwards as a treat. Like a little reward for the challenging sessions! But at no point did I think I couldn't do this. There was never any doubt about me continuing, or any thinking, 'Yeah, this isn't really for me after all.' I have never felt like I couldn't accomplish something or go through with something when I put my mind to it and focus. And I was focused.

Of course, there are always some things that have to give and that was stuff back at St Peter's. If everyone else was talking about the end-of-year graduation prom, for example, what they were going to wear, who'd be going with who, I would just sit and listen knowing that I was going to miss that. But then again, I still thought what I was doing was pretty cool. I was going along to high-performance training, England training; the prestige of that outweighed school social events for me and although it did suck to miss out, it's all part of the sacrifice that young athletes often speak about.

And leaving school at lunchtime while everyone still had an afternoon of lessons to come was always quite cool. Waving to my mates as I left. 'Where you going, Geva?' was the normal shout. 'Gotta go England training!' would be my grinning response. I felt like I gained a lot of respect from other pupils and teachers as it was unheard of at the school, a pupil playing for England, so in a sense I was probably treated a bit like a star. It made me blush, and I like to think I was usually quite modest, but if not Mum would bring me right down to earth. She definitely kept me grounded. 'You're a small fish in a big pond' was her favourite saying. And she was right. Yeah, it was cool, I had played for England. So what?! Now I had to crack on and prove I deserved a place on the team. So I had no chance of feeling too smug for too long! The training was also no place for bragging. Lyn's training sessions were full on and I had it hammered into me every time: 'Do not cut corners, Geva!' It was her favourite thing to say but it sank in – there was no substitute for hard work and practice.

After about three months it was clear that driving up and down to training so many times a week wasn't the most time-effective way, and so it was agreed that I would stay up in Bath for the week instead. Mum would drive me up to Bath on a Sunday evening and I'd stay with Lyn for the week until Mum collected me on the Friday morning. I would then go straight into school and hand in all the coursework I had done that week and get more work from the teachers for the following week. I was studying for my A levels, living away from home, and training three times a day for England Netball selection.

I probably didn't much appreciate my teachers at the time but, bloody hell, when I look back at the preparation and time they gave me, I am beyond grateful. They would often stay late after school and meet me in the detention room with all the so-called naughty kids to go through work that I had missed and stuff I was going to miss the following week. So not only did they make sure I had all the right material and study sheets, they would have had to prepare what they were teaching the following week in class in order to give it to me the Friday before. Credit to those teachers – Mike Spackman, thank you!

My time in Bath wasn't that fun, to be honest. I was staying with the coach, after all, and you can imagine how on edge that would make you. I was young, I wasn't at home, and I didn't feel I could relax. Home should be a place where you can switch off and forget about training or netball, which is a bit hard to do when you are living with the England Netball coach! However uncomfortable I might have felt, Lyn's comments had the best intentions. She wanted to make me a better athlete, a better student, a better person . . . I just didn't fully appreciate it as a teenager!

So my week would pretty much run like this: Monday to Thursday I would train early in the mornings, then when I had finished I would go to the library and do some school-work. Then there would be more training in the afternoon before I would head back to Lyn's house and study some more in the evening. She lived at the bottom of this really steep hill, Claverton Down, and she used to tell me that if I wanted a lift up the hill for training I would have to be ready to leave at 4.30 a.m. Or I could walk it and get an extra hour in bed and get away with leaving at 5.30 a.m. So some mornings I would try to get a lift; it meant a horribly early start but at least I didn't have to climb what seemed like Everest with a backpack full of books and training gear. Other mornings I was like, 'Screw it, I can cope with the walk, I want another hour in bed!' But oh my goodness, that walk. I used to come up with some ingenious ways to get up the hill in my head while I was stomping up it with what seemed like the heaviest bag in the world. I could stick out my thumb and try to hitchhike, or if I'd had a skateboard I could have tied a rope round a car's bumper and got pulled up! Anything to take my mind off walking up the hill! So that was a pretty intense time but I knew it would ultimately be worth it. If working hard meant I could secure a place in the Commonwealth Games for later that year, I would do all that I could.

And in June that year, I was named one of the twelve in the squad. All the hard work had paid off.

6 COMING OF AGE AT THE COMMONWEALTH GAMES

'We have picked the people who are playing the best netball in the country at the moment.'

Waimarama Taumaunu,
England Netball Performance Director

WHEN I first got into the England squad, netball was Lottery-funded and one of the programmes we had was called Sporting Champions. The idea was that elite athletes or well-known local or national sporting heroes would go out and visit kids in schools and sports clubs and community centres to tell them their story. Sometimes I think children believe you wake up in an England kit and don't always see that we started off just like them with only ambition and dreams, so it was great to chat to lots of different children about our pathway and give advice or motivation for theirs. I would talk about my netball training, what I would go through day to day, how I got into the sport, what other sports I enjoyed doing. I loved being involved in this campaign; this was exactly what I enjoyed most, motivating and enthusing the younger generation. I was still only young myself and so I think I made a real connection with the majority of the kids I had the pleasure to meet. I was happy to travel all over the south coast and even caught a ferry over to the Isle of Wight one day to speak to children at a school over there. I enjoyed sharing my story. What I did was bigger than just me, and if I could inspire people or give them a glimpse of all the things I did, that was cool. Not that I was expecting them to take everything on board but at the end of the day it might give them some insight, it might help them find a way, help them on their journey. Sometimes hearing from someone who has done everything you want to do and has turned out OK does help, whether they would ultimately go down the sporting path like me or whether I just gave them ideas about how to balance things at school or maintain relationships with friends.

I was no public speaker, though, and at the time I didn't have my story down; I just spoke from the heart about things I had experienced, difficulties I had come across, the exciting people I had met. Kids seem to get that. I have a lot of time for youngsters; it's probably why I decided to start studying for a teaching degree. I would always go back to my old school when I had the chance and help out in a PE lesson or something. It was nice to give something back. The point I think I am trying to make is that while I was living and breathing netball and focusing on my career and on playing for England, there was a whole new generation about to embark on the same thoughts and decisions and possibilities that I had faced and I thought it was important to show them the same encouragement and support that I got.

The announcement that I had made the squad for the 2002 Commonwealth Games in Manchester came in June. After training us hard in Bath for the previous five months, Lyn took the England team on an intensive seven-match ten-day tour in Australia. Timing-wise for the team, it was perfect to get some good match practice in against the reigning champions as well as two of the top National League teams.

I had been playing netball for Team Bath since I started training and living with Lyn. It was one of the top premier-ship teams in the South West. Before that I had been with Team Surrey and before that East Dorset Counties. After my first game with the senior England side I was told I had to play for a higher division than the one I was in with Bournemouth, in my home county. We were playing in Division Five and thrashing anyone who came up against us. England Netball told me I had to be playing in Division One or Two and no lower. One of the ladies on the England team, Lyn Carpenter, was playing for Surrey at the time and she took me under her wing a bit and encouraged me to join Surrey, which I did for a season. It was a bit of a trek, travelling to Epsom once a week, and I don't know if I just didn't enjoy it because of the journey or if I just didn't like it, but I didn't think long about joining Team Bath – it helped that my friend Pam Cookey was also part of the team – and Gloucestershire was to be my new county team. I later moved over to HNC, Hucclecote Netball Club, with Gloucestershire, as they were in Division One. Everything was just slowly finding its place, everything went into some sort of order without being too overwhelming for me or my family.

Team Bath actually had three players selected to form part of a 'development squad', a team that would be available in the training camp two weeks prior to the Games. It was their job to provide competition for the teams who would be playing in the Games and were looking for final match-play opportunities. The development squad also acted as training partners for the England team and it was great to see some teammates and girls from other clubs having that opportunity to play against the best in the world before the big event.

There was a real buzz in Manchester leading up to the Games. We were there prior to the opening ceremony and I remember wandering around the city, checking out the shops, as we mostly did in our free time during camp. On a rare afternoon off from training, I was out and about with Amanda Newton, Sonia Mkoloma and a few other girls when we bumped into Tracey Neville's brother. Tracey is my current England coach and was one of my teammates back then, and it was her older brother Gary we saw, the famous Manchester United footballer. Tracey is from a great sporty family; as well as Gary there is her twin Phil, who is also a former Premier League and England footballer. Gary is particularly close to one of his former teammates, David Beckham, and both lads are very well-known in the area, having played football for Manchester United and England. That afternoon we hadn't officially entered the athletes' village yet and we just wanted to leave the hotel and stretch our legs a bit and get some fresh air. So there we were, just wandering around the shops, and we bumped into Gary. We started chatting about the upcoming Games and he asked us how we were feeling. He was very chatty and interested in what we thought our chances were. And to be honest, I think we were a bit bemused that he would just wander around and not get hounded by a million fans.

'I'm normally all right,' he said, 'but this one over here,' pointing to David Beckham, 'stands out like a sore thumb!' And we all turned and there was David, less than two metres away, in a bright red cap and bright red trainers. It was so funny. There was no way he wasn't going to get noticed, he was like a beacon! But he was equally friendly and encouraging and it was a surreal but cool moment for us. Gary and Phil were very supportive of their sister and Gary would often come along to international matches to cheer Tracey on, bringing his pal David on more than a few occasions.

And then it was time to experience my first Commonwealth Games. The first of five Games, as it would turn out, but at the time I had never experienced anything like it before and it was beyond exciting. Manchester had been preparing for this for a couple of years and the atmosphere was unreal; there was a real thrill about playing on home turf and the anticipation was high. England had won a bronze medal at the previous games in Kuala Lumpur four years ago and half the team playing this year had been part of that squad, including Tracey. Pam and I were in the team and there was a bit of a buzz about us, two seventeen-year-old girls hoping to make an impact. I remember seeing an interview with Waimarama Taumaunu when she was asked about the squad, which mixed the experienced girls with us newbies. 'We have picked the people who are playing the best netball in the country at the moment,' she said, and I was proud that that included me! I really felt part of the squad and I knew I would be getting some action on court even though I wouldn't be part of the starting seven. I was probably the third of four defenders in line but that would mean some court time. England Netball would normally work tournaments by having a strong starting seven play for at least half the game before they would bring on fresh legs and rest the top players for after the group stages, when the serious business really began. It gave everyone a good amount of court time and you weren't tiring out all your starting seven. We had Canada, Sri Lanka, Wales and New Zealand in our group and we felt all would be easy wins except the world number-two team, the Silver Ferns.

My godmother and Mum's best friend Jackie lives in North Wales so Mum stayed over with her and did the commute in to see our games. She was there for the whole thing, and it was great as she actually got to see me play for England this time!

The opening ceremony was on 25 July and our first game was the following day against Canada. We then faced Sri Lanka on 27 July, Wales on the 28th and New Zealand on the 29th.

The athletes' village, where all the athletes in the Games slept and ate and prepared, was just unbelievable. Someone once described it as the best all-inclusive holiday you can ever go on and that was exactly what it felt like. Everything was free, so you'd walk around and there'd be little food stalls and vending machines and you could just help yourself to stuff. And then in the main food hall there were different stalls set up with food from all over the world. So you took your pick as to what national cuisine you fancied – Indian, Asian, British, Italian . . . it was just mind-blowing.

People call the Commonwealth Games the 'friendly games' and you can see why. Everyone is very happy and sociable and giving lots of smiles – at least before the competitions start. You pass nations who are playing in other events and wave and say; 'Hi! How are you?' But when you spot another netballing team, you try to get your game face on and give them a serious look. I should point out, however, that nowadays I have either played or am still playing with girls from other countries, so not only do I stop and say hello, I'm usually there for a good half an hour having a natter!

Being part of Team England was pretty incredible. You weren't just this tight-knit netball family any more; there was a huge extended family here ready and waiting to encourage and support and cheer you on. You were more than a netball team, you were part of Team England and you were wearing the kit with pride. Whenever you walked around and spotted someone else with the same gear you gave a little head-nod, a smile, an acknowledgement of this powerhouse you were now part of. It was one of the most memorable things I took from the Games, that feeling of being appreciated as an athlete by other athletes in this amazing family. And being on home soil gave Team England an extra boost; this was our territory, we walked around with an extra air of confidence. This was home to us. Good luck to everyone else. That isn't to say that walking around among some of the most iconic sporting heroes you have seen on the TV at the Olympics wasn't mind-blowing. It was incredible to think you could bump into a world-famous athlete in the same food hall or wandering around the village. That feeling doesn't go either; each Common-wealth Games is the same, the same appreciation that you are in the presence of athletes at the top of their game in their chosen sport, and it is truly memorable. I would love to see netball recognised as an Olympic sport – to bring it to a bigger audience, put it on a bigger stage, would be phenomenal. I know it probably won't happen in my playing career but perhaps it will in my lifetime. I think the major problem is that there are too many sports already part of the Olympics and it's only really played by women. At the 2000 Sydney Olympics there was talk of it being included as Australia were the world champions, but the other three big Olympic nations, America, Russia and China, didn't play it at an elite level and until they do it is unlikely to be included. Any athlete would love their sport to be in the Olympics so it is frustrating. But for the time being, the Commonwealth Games was proving to be a magical experience.

Team England headquarters were very impressive; we had our own little apartment complex. There was a main entrance area as you walked in and then each sport had their own little apartments and sections. There was a guy on the reception who would send you in the right direction for laundry or for the massage rooms. He sat behind a big desk and forgive my youthfulness but I remember that on that desk was a massive vase. I thought there were sweets in it at first and it was only when I went right up for a look at what sort of sweets that I realised it was full of colourful condoms! 'Right, OK,' I thought. 'That is why it's called the friendly games!' It wasn't embarrassing, it was more just so funny that there was this ginormous vase in the Team England reception for everyone to see and help themselves from! And in the second week of the Games, in the vending machines that had previously been giving out Gatorade, soft drinks and water there were now bottles of beer. I was shocked! I would like to say here that the other Games I have been to haven't been anything like this. There was no massive vase of johnnies on display; if you wanted protection you had to ask for it. It does seem weird, doesn't it, like something from the seventies! It wasn't something I told Mum – she didn't need to know there was free beer and contraception!

There was another surreal moment for me when the Queen came to visit the athletes' village during the competition. I am a huge fan of hers and the royal family; in fact, I have a bit of an obsession with the monarchy, and so seeing her in real life was a massive deal for me. As I am sure it would be for anyone! Word went round that she was there and that she was in the food hall and then, of course, everyone in the village wanted to try to get to see her and it was a massive scramble. I managed to get within about five metres of her and to see her in person was so exciting. She was tiny. She only had a few delegates with her and she was looking and smiling at everyone. Her being there was an extra-magical moment. I think I have become more of a royalist since living in Australia because they absolutely adore the royal family over there. I love the history, I love the traditions; I find it all so fascinating and so you can imagine my pure excitement of being just a few feet away from the Queen of England!

But back to the Games themselves. England had a bit of expectation around them; we had won bronze four years ago, would we be able to match that or go one or two better with the home crowd behind us? Sadly not. We performed as expected in the group stages, beating Wales, Canada and

Sri Lanka quite comfortably before losing to New Zealand, which meant we finished second in our group. We then had to compete in the play-offs between the four teams that finished second and third in the two groups. We played South Africa, who had come third in their group, and Jamaica played Wales, who had finished third in our group. We managed to hold our own against South Africa, the SPAR Proteas, beating them 55–40. And then it was time for the semi-finals. The mood in the team was positive but we were up against Australia, the reigning champions, and we lost by nearly ten goals. We ended up losing in the bronze medal play-off against Jamaica too, by two goals. That was hard. We were so close yet not quite there. Although we came away from those Commonwealth Games with nothing, I had a mind full of incredible memories. It might have been youthful ignorance or determination or a fire in my belly but I vowed that this wasn't going to be my only Commonwealth Championship. I was seventeen years old and hungry for better results.

We were back in Australia and New Zealand later that year on another tour and test-match series. It stands out in my memory because we met with the England rugby team while we were in New Zealand. It was the year before they won the World Cup and it was just so cool meeting the likes of Jonny Wilkinson and Martin Johnson. I have a great deal of respect for rugby players, maybe in part thanks to my PE teacher Patrick but also due to the incredible pressure they put on their bodies and how they just knuckle down and get on with their games. They have a job to do and they do it. The England rugby team is a bit like the netball team; there is a bit of national interest in it but nothing on the same level as football. I think this works well for us and them – we both just get on with things. We have a job to do, we want to do it well. I was on a netball court in England the following year playing a match when it was announced that England had won the rugby World Cup. There was a massive cheer as the news came over the tannoy! Then we just carried on, buoyed by the victory.

The year 2003 was a big one for the England rugby team in the World Cup but would we have the same result in our World Championship? It was being held in Kingston in Jamaica for ten days from 10 July. I had the small matter of completing my A levels first, however, and – as always – it wasn't straightforward for me. I was with the England squad on a test series in New Zealand when I was due to sit my exams and so while all my mates were back home in England, all sitting round nervously together in the sports hall, I was in New Zealand sitting nervously with six or seven strangers from all over the world, all doing their own exams, in a small classroom at the university.

It was all very expertly done; the school had posted the sealed envelope with my exam in and the envelope was opened in front of me to show it hadn't been tampered with. I only did two A levels, geography and sports studies, not the more usual three. I did originally start with three but I had to drop one in the second year. It was too much trying to fit in study and travelling and training and something had to give. So on this day, all the other girls on the team were out sightseeing or shopping or having lunch somewhere and there was me, sitting in a strange classroom about to sit my A level exams. But I did it, and I am pleased I did.

England Netball took the build-up to the World Championships very seriously. They wanted us to be as prepared as we possibly could be as we were playing in Jamaica in July, in extremely hot conditions. It was decided that we should train at the University of Hertfordshire in Hatfield as they had a heat chamber we could use. They had exercise bikes in the heat chamber and so we'd take it in turns, in groups of about five or six, to go in, use the bikes and do passes against the wall before swapping over. We did heaps of work in that heat chamber, making sure we did all we could to prepare ourselves for the climate of Jamaica. We took it very seriously and when we went home after the training we were advised to use our local saunas too so we could keep ourselves acclimatised. I went along to the David Lloyd gym round the corner from Mum's house and used the sauna. I took with me a list of exercises they had given us – ten squats, ten sit-ups, fast-feet running on the spot – all designed to lift our heart rates in a humid environment.

And the coaches kept drumming into us about keeping ourselves hydrated; we must keep drinking all the time. England Netball even invested in these ice vests for us to wear. They were a bit like buoyancy aids but they were full of ice packs, and you'd put them over your dress. They would help to cool down our body temperature and the aim was to put them on between quarters.

When it came to flying out to Jamaica you could say we felt pretty prepared for the temperature and how our bodies would cope with playing in the heat. We weren't exactly smug but we felt like we had done our homework and it wouldn't be our surroundings that would let us down. You can imagine our faces when we turned up at the sports arena for our first match and it was bloody freezing because of the air-conditioning! Seriously, what a waste of time all that intense heat training had been! We actually found it quite funny – we were expecting it to be an oven and we end up freezing our tits off! It sort of summed up England Netball at that point. I shared a room with Sonia Mkoloma, who was GD to my GK. The first night a bloody fruitbat somehow got into our room and we couldn't get it out! I can laugh about it now, but it was traumatic at the time and neither of us got any sleep.

It was another disappointing championship for us as we came fourth. Having made it through our group stages, we played against South Africa in the quarter-finals and Sonia and I were working well as a defensive partnership, turning over the ball and sending it back down the other end, but our error rate as a team was high, simple passing and catching mistakes or missed shots. It was so frustrating; we had our hearts set on the semi-finals and playing against Australia and we were struggling to get the finish. Australia, New Zealand, England and Jamaica were considered the top four teams in the world and the other three seemed to be doing what was expected of them but we were struggling. I remember distinctly one passage of play, in the final quarter of that game. The scores were neck and neck – well, South Africa might have been up by one goal – and Sonia and I had managed to turn over the ball and send it back down our end. Someone threw it to our goal shooter and it went right through her hands and off the back line. That's the thing with shooters, when a game goes right they take all the glory but when it goes wrong, the finger of blame is pointed directly at them. Sonia pounded the ground with both hands, shouting her head off in frustration. It was a frustration I felt too, of course, but we had to keep our heads in the moment and keep providing opportunities. Sonia and I were a formidable team and eager to show that we were potential starters for the team. We had been working on our defence partnership once a week in Brunel before this championship and I remember saying to her as she took her annoyance out on the court, 'It's OK, Sonia, we can get it back, it's our game.' You have to have that belief, that fighting-to-the-end spirit, especially as a defender, because quite often games are lost in the final quarter, in those dying moments as the players start to lose momentum. Sonia and I were both fighting for every second, as were all the girls on court at the time, and I just needed to remind her of this. 'Just be cool, this is what we love to do, we love to turn over the ball.'

It didn't help that the lights went off in that game as well. You couldn't make it up. Jamaica were playing Australia on the other court and I think the rumour was that someone had done this on purpose to help the Jamaicans. We don't know if it was planned or not but the lights went off for a period of time and when they finally came back on – they were on a generator so it took a good five minutes for it to all kick back in again – there was a dispute over where play should start again. It was all a bit controversial but we ended up winning by the skin of our teeth – but then went on to lose against Australia 37–45 in the semi-final. That led us to face the host nation in the bronze medal match and I ended up coming on in the third or fourth quarter as their goal shooter was just destroying us. I was pleased to have got on court but we ended up losing that match too. We just weren't quite firing on all cylinders yet, we weren't clicking as a team. I remember watching Australia and New Zealand play each other in the final and it was an epic battle. The Silver Ferns centre got sent off for too many contacts or too many offsides and was off the court for about two minutes. The score was neck and neck at that point and when she came back on, she stole some balls and New Zealand ended up winning. It was such an amazing game to watch. This was the level I wanted to play at. It was phenomenal to watch those girls in action; I was in awe.

After the World Cup disappointment I took part in some county matches with Gloucestershire and test matches in Loughborough. I was preparing for the 2005 World Youth Cup, which is basically the same as the World Cup but for the under-twenty-one squad. Having played for the senior squad in the World Cup, I was now scheduled to play for the under-twenty-ones too and get familiar with my team-mates. I was nineteen years old and netball had taken over my life completely. I had finished my studies, I was doing a bit of work for Dorset's Sports Council as a sports rep coach and it all fitted in nicely around training.

Each year I would have to try out for the England squad. They often say it's hard to make the squad, harder to make the team, and even harder to make the court, and it's true. Each time you go in front of the selectors it is around my birthday in September. And again, it would involve a day of fitness testing and a day of match play. All the selectors are out and making notes and watching. I think I got to a point where I looked at it as a nice way of catching up with everybody. We would often say to ourselves, 'Why are we even doing this? The coaches know who they want to pick half the time, they know what combination they want, why do they want to burn us out for the weekend?' But it is a rite of passage; they make us do it and we do. I have never taken it for granted and definitely in the early days I was very grateful for the opportunities that came my way. I was never complacent that I was being selected and some friends of mine weren't. Girls I had got to know at different competitions or test matches, who were in the team and then the next moment weren't. I have been very fortunate not to have ever gone through deselection with the England team at trials. My time of not being allowed to play for England was going to come in a few years but I was never not selected through ability. I worked bloody hard to stay in that team and I am pleased that although I was still young, my maturity and passion to play for England was clear to see. It did become difficult when the try-outs were moved around the country – sometimes they were in Sheffield, sometimes they were in Loughborough, and you'd travel up with a group of girls all hoping to get a place on the squad. And then of course England Netball went through different stages of letting us know who they had selected – sometimes you stood up and were told, other times you got a letter and you could choose to open that letter there and then or later on.

I remember once, driving back from try-outs with five of us crammed into the car, we started opening letters on the way and only two of us had been selected. It is the most awkward feeling because obviously you are completely elated that you are part of Team England but you feel for the person sitting in the car next to you who has gone through exactly the same things – busted their arse just like you – to prove they deserve a place and not been selected. In those early years of being part of the selection process I think the coaches saw some potential in me and wanted to keep me around. I was a quick and eager learner and I was a team player and, although I wasn't having much on-court time still, I was contributing to the team.

And so it was that I stayed as part of the senior squad and the under-twenty-one squad and after a tough three- or four-week tour with the seniors in Australia, I then met up with the under-twenty-ones, who had come out to Oz to prepare for the World Youth Cup in 2005.

They were headed to the AIS, the Australian Institute of Sport, to play against the Australian under-twenty-ones. I was exhausted and feeling very run down from coming off one tour and going straight into another one. It always seems to be a thing with me that after every tour I get a bit poorly and suffer. It's amazing what performing does to you; it keeps you going all the way through and then literally a week or two after a test series I'll get a cold for a couple of days. I was really run down when we were at the AIS and I picked up a chest infection. It got to the point that the physios were having to bang me on the back to clear the mucus from my chest. I used to come off at the end of each quarter and they'd be banging my back around to give me a bit of a breather and then I'd run back on again. All of this was at the side of the court and it got to the point where they were knocking my back and freeing up my mucus so much that I started to cough some of it up. I then had to have a spittoon at the side of the court, which was disgusting, but it meant I could carry on playing! I'd like to say I got a lot of sympathy from my teammates but I think they found it quite funny. It also didn't help that one of my teammates, Naida Hutchinson, had an uncanny knack for doing impressions and impersonations of the umpires and she had us all in stitches that game, which for me wasn't great as it set me off coughing again!

7 GETTING THE JOB DONE

'Somewhere behind the athlete you've become and the hours of practice and the coaches who have pushed you is a little girl who fell in love with the game and never looked back. Play for her.'   Mia Hamm

I MIGHT have been suffering during the preparation, but I was firing on all cylinders by the time I joined the under-twenty-one squad on a plane heading to the 2005 World Youth Cup. It was being held in Fort Lauderdale in Florida and the best thing was that my mum and Raoul flew out to watch me play. They were staying with a friend from Bournemouth, Vicky Simmonds, who now lived in Fort Lauderdale.

America wasn't the most obvious place to hold a big netball tournament as they hadn't really heard of the sport and I think people were confused when they saw us walking around as a team. We often got comments like, 'Oh, you're here to play basketball? No? Volleyball?' The World Youth

Cup is the pinnacle of netball competition for emerging players and features twenty countries competing across the five INF (International Netball Federation) regions: Africa, the Americas, Asia, Europe and Oceania.

Whether I had an extra fire in my belly having come away disappointed from the World Championships in Jamaica two years before I'm not sure, but my mentality was strong – we could do this! And we started off our campaign in that frame of mind, winning our group stages. We played Jamaica in the semi-finals. I was a starter for the under-twenty-ones and sometimes I would be swapped in as goal defence. We managed to beat Jamaica in the semis, winning 52–48, and I was about to enter my first gold medal finals match with an England dress on. I can't speak for any of the other girls but in my experience when you are faced with a gold medal final, you have to have the desire to win, to go for gold. I know I did but it still burns me to this day that when it came to that match, playing New Zealand for a gold medal, we didn't do ourselves justice. It seemed a lot of the girls in the squad were content with the fact that they had already come away with – at the very least – a silver medal. I genuinely felt that when we went out on court in the first quarter it was all there for the taking, the whole tournament, and we just didn't take it. I couldn't help but feel that the girls didn't feel they could win gold. The mood was different; everyone had been so prepared and focused for the semi-final match and when we won it the whole squad just seemed to relax and not have the same care about going into a gold medal final. We should have been even more focused! Everyone stayed up that little bit later the night before, there was a little more messing around and carefree attitude than before. I couldn't fathom that; perhaps it was because we weren't used to competing at the very top, or maybe I had an increased air of maturity, having been in the seniors and knowing what getting to a final would mean, and the under-twenty-ones didn't have that same hunger. Rather than think, 'Sweet, we have propelled ourselves to silver, let's propel ourselves all the way,' the mentality seemed to be more, 'Cool, we've got a silver medal!' I got moved from goalkeeper to goal defence in that final quarter and we ended up losing by four goals.

It's funny but I still feel the same frustration I felt then and this was nearly fifteen years ago! So we ended up with a silver medal and the best thing about the tournament was having Mum and Raoul with me and us all taking a little holiday afterwards. We went to Disney World and Universal Studios and all the usual tourist hotspots. It was nice to slip away and have a bit of a distraction. It just didn't sit well with me, that attitude, and although I didn't vent to my teammates I had a chance to chat it out with Mum and Raoul. And then it was time to make the most of our holiday and some much-needed family time!

When we came back to England after America it was all about preparing for the Commonwealth Games, which were being held in Melbourne in March the following year. I am pretty sure we had another series tour out there in preparation before the Games themselves. Barring the 2018 Games when we took the gold medal (I have to mention this at least a few times!), the 2006 Melbourne Games were probably my favourite. I was named in the twelve-woman squad and although I was still one of the youngest, I was already one of the most capped. It was a great feeling. I think I commented in one newspaper interview that it meant I didn't have to carry the netball bags any more! And it was an awesome Games in terms of its surroundings and vibe and the sun was out and it felt like everyone was buzzing. All the tickets to the netball matches were sold out in the initial ballot as the sport was so popular, so we felt really important! I was twenty-one years old now and I feel I had matured a little bit since my last Games. We made it through our group stages fairly easily, losing to New Zealand, who were also in our group. We played really well too. I was getting a bit more court time and things were going well. Sonia and I were like partners in crime; we worked as a solid unit and our slightly different defensive style was getting us noticed. The *New Zealand Herald* wrote: 'while defenders of similar height and stature often grapple with speed and control, Mentor and Mkoloma seem to whip their tentacles out and connect with the ball at lightning speed'. It was true, we both knew we had our height and we had our timing and we know we can do it, which is why we go for it. I suppose I have to thank trampolining for that. Being friends with Sonia on and off the court certainly helped too and I think having Lyn and

Waimarama, a former defensive player, helped us work on our game. Waimarama was quite scary, don't get me wrong – you made sure you listened to her, that's for sure. But she was a former Silver Ferns player and we benefited from having her on our side.

We lost out to Australia in the quarter-finals by eight goals and were due to face Jamaica in the bronze-medal play-offs. It was a goal-for-goal match and we were determined not to lose out in the same way as at the previous Games. We stayed focused and strong and ended up winning 53–52. We got bronze! And it was a gorgeous medal too. Some of them can be quite plain but this one felt and looked beautiful.

After the Games Rachel Dunn, who was our goal shooter, and I decided to go travelling around Australia for a bit. I think I probably fell in love with the country on our travels. Normally when you come over for a series or a tournament you don't get much chance to sightsee other than in the area you are playing. Rachel and I decided we wanted to fit in as much as we could and so we backpacked in style. We used contacts we had made from being in the country before and we went to Sydney, Alice Springs, Uluru, the Whitsundays . . . it was such an adventure. It was great to really explore the country without the pressure of sport. Being a shooter, Rachel is quite tall too and people would stop us and ask if we were netballers. We said that yes, we were, and explained that we had just played in the Com Games and people were so interested and wanted to talk to us. Nothing like when I was in Florida the year before! And even in England, you can travel around and people don't really pick up on who you are.

It was still two years away from me making the move to Australia but I think that stint travelling and exploring with Rachel was my first indication that I was falling in love with the country. But back to England we went and back to training for the World Championships, which were going to be held in Auckland, New Zealand in 2007.

I was very excited that Mum and Raoul were coming out to watch the World Cup. I missed Raoul a fair bit when I was away at tournaments and it was great to know he and Mum were watching. I owe a lot to Raoul; he often kept me company when I was travelling up to Bath for training two or three times a week. I could drive now, so Mum didn't have to make the journey, but I would get lonely and I could sometimes persuade him, in exchange for a KFC Twister on the way home, to come up and back to training with me. I remember almost pleading with him to come with me and saying that I would make it worth his while. It's still a thing for me now; any long drive I have to do I will almost always beg Raoul to join me if he can. I'm not needy, I just appreciate the company! While I trained, he would shoot some hoops or something at the side of the court or just entertain himself and then I would get him the KFC I'd promised. He would then be supposed to try to keep me awake on the way home, although most of the time he would end up falling asleep himself – which didn't matter; having the company was all I needed. It seemed a fair trade and I liked having him with me. Well, most of the time, but not when he puked everywhere in my car when we were probably about fifteen minutes away from home! He'd looked a little off since we'd left Bath and I asked him if he was all right. He looked at me, looked at the road, looked at me again and vomited everywhere. And I mean *everywhere* – the footwell, the gearstick, the hand-brake, all over me, all over the dashboard. I couldn't really get that cross with him as I was the one who had wanted him there, but he could have done a nice tidy pile of sick! I had to have the car completely valeted after that and I even had a special lemon car bomb exploded in it after-wards, but I still couldn't get rid of the smell for about a month!

During the World Championships I don't think he was that interested in watching many of the games, but I was getting more court time and my mum was there at every match. She gets really nervous about watching me play so she started to develop this habit, which she is now well known for. She would watch the first two quarters and then walk out of the stadium; she couldn't watch the remainder of the game. When we lost out to Australia in the semi-finals and faced Jamaica in the bronze medal play-offs again, it was too much for her. She had seen the relation-ship England had with Jamaica over the years and didn't think it was fair. Bless my mum, sport isn't fair and that was as much for her to learn as me, I suppose. To her it seemed that they would come through and steal the medals right at the end of the match, which is why she couldn't watch the final quarter. I would like to say that the bronze-medal play-off was different this time round but they snatched victory again, by one goal. It was heartbreaking but character-building and like with most tournaments, we had lots to take and learn from it. There was one funny thing that happened in that tournament – I say funny, but at the time we were a little panicked (I was definitely stressed, I hate being late). Sonia and I almost missed a complete training session. We were sharing a room and were running late to catch the team bus that was going to take us to the training venue. We got downstairs just as the bus was pulling away and chased it, banging on the sides and back for it to stop. It was so funny as we could see the girls on there chatting away and not having a clue what was happening outside! We couldn't get anyone's attention and the bus drove off. It was like in the movies, the bus driving off into the sunset and us looking at each other with a look of 'What the . . .?!' on our faces. But there we were, left behind. We actually saw Kath Harby-Williams, an Australian player, walking along the pavement on her way to the venue and we were like, 'Eeek! We've just been left behind!' She just shook her head, laughed at us, and continued on her way. We ran back to the hotel reception and got them to call a taxi for us and we headed after the bus. Thankfully, when you get to a practice venue people strap themselves up and the shooters go and shoot a few goals to warm up before the coach calls everyone over to commence the session. We strapped ourselves up in the taxi so that when we arrived, albeit a little frazzled, we made it in time before they wondered where the hell we were!

Mum decided that a road trip around New Zealand was what we all needed and she hired a wicked camper van as our very own tour bus. She picked me up from the team hotel, her driving, my brother in the middle and me next to him. I needed to forget another disappointing tournament and Mum knew this would help. She has always been there to pick up the pieces. She was also good at giving me a reality check and when we stopped at our first campsite and woke up the next day to the most beautiful scenery and dolphins playing in the bay below, I did think to myself, netball? It's just a game. As frustrated as I felt – as much as that feeling of hurt engulfed my mind – I found perspective. I was resilient. I had fight in me. Life goes on; you grow, you learn and you keep going. There is life outside of the sport. When you are in that bubble of post-match frustration it is very hard to get on with things but then you do and you realise, actually, things are OK. You can be thankful for where you are and the opportunities you have experienced.

It hurts when I lose. I don't get angry or lose my temper, I just ache with hurt. In my heart I know we should have done much better, so a lot of it is self-pity mixed in with frustration. And it can be hard to deal with. Immediately after a game, you try to do exactly the same things you'd do if you had won. Everyone knew that we weren't unfortunate; we lost. And that is the important thing in sport, you can't beat around the bush. Either we played shit or we allowed the opposition to get on top of us, or we didn't execute when it mattered. You have to be open and honest about what went wrong or you will never improve. It is never bad luck, there are some unlucky calls perhaps but I'm a firm believer that you make your own luck. So we do break it down in the debriefing room and we look at the game and we then pick up where our areas of concern are. Maybe it was our centre pass conversion rate or our shot-to-goal percentage, or maybe we didn't turn over enough balls in defence . . . we really make sure we all know the areas we didn't nail so we know that these are areas to target and work on next time. However raw you feel after a defeat, you have to keep it practical. You have to try to keep emotion out of it. It does help to try to be precise and have a focus. It is emotional, of course it is. You wouldn't be human if you didn't feel anything, and those emotions, for me, are the motivation. They are the drive to make the changes and put in the extra hours and keep pushing for a win. One of the obvious things with team sports is that it's very easy to blame your team-mates and dissect their performance as well as yours – and yes, it can be frustrating when a teammate who you know is capable of great things doesn't perform. But we've all been there, we've all had bad days at the office. The annoyance comes when they can't recognise that they have underper-formed, because the first step in improving is recognition.

You've got all of these things coming into your head after a game and that is the hardest thing with a team sport. Obviously it is great when you're winning but sometimes winning masks the cracks and when you are losing you see things more clearly. I often think you can learn more from your losses than your wins. Don't get me wrong, I hate to lose, but I can see the bigger picture.

I guess that is the intriguing part of sport – you can really identify people's characters, how they deal with things, when you watch them lose. I actually like looking at the behaviours of the teams or individuals that lose. I think the reactions they initially display are a true reflection of what it means to them but, more importantly, how they'll learn from it. I look at how they support the team, how they strive to rectify or improve their game. And that is the important bit. You have to keep the same sort of mannerisms and behaviour whether you win or lose. And then you identify the areas that need to improve. And if you recognise that there is never a 'perfect' game, there is always room for improvement, you'll continually make yourself a better player.

All the teams I have been involved with are pretty good like that; there is no one that is delusional with what has happened after a match. Whether they are at fault individually or as a unit. I like to be around everyone after a loss and keep the focus positive. 'OK, it's done. Let's look at the bigger picture.' I keep things level-headed and I keep plugging the fact that everything happens for a reason. It wasn't our time and, as crap as it is, that is the way it is.

I try to be supportive and talk about the effort everyone has put in and it's only afterwards, when I step away and see my mum and my brother and have time to deal with it and reflect, that I probably think about my own perform- ance, think about the lost opportunities, and that is when my frustrations kick in.

Years later, in the 2014 Commonwealth Games, this mental approach helped us deal with a horrible loss. Yes, you can isolate particular things that happened in a game – like a bad pass or a missed shot – but you can't put the loss down to just that. We all have things that happen throughout a game but it just so happened that at a critical moment in our last-round game against the Silver Ferns, one teammate, Kadeen Corbin, who was GA, made a terrible pass that got intercepted by Laura Langman, the Ferns centre, and the ball whizzed down their shooting end. I couldn't stop it and they scored to equalise and then scored again – we lost the game by one goal after having control for fifty-nine minutes and thirty seconds. We were all gutted and of course there was a mixture of emotions – frustration, anger, sadness. I guess Kadeen felt it was all her fault but the blame can't be placed just on her shoulders. One mistake doesn't make a loss. I knew she was hurting after the game and I made sure I went up to her and consoled her. She was in tears. We were all upset but we were realistic as well – netball is a team sport. We win together, we lose together, we hurt together. We ride the emotions – the highs and the lows – as a team.

But back to 2008. Actually, let me take you back to a phone call that Mum and I were in on in September 2007, a phone call with the Adelaide Thunderbirds CEO, their head coach Jane Woodlands-Thompson and netball guru Todd Miller. There was going to be a new premier league starting in Australia and New Zealand that would be contested between five teams from Australia and five teams from New Zealand. There would be sixty-nine matches held annually, played over seventeen weeks, and Todd wanted the Thunderbirds, one of the five Australian teams, to sign me. He had spotted me before the World Championships and knew that if Adelaide Thunderbirds waited until after that tournament, I would be receiving offers from most – if not all – of the teams. I was twenty-three years old and I was about to embark on the biggest move of my career.

Signing with the Adelaide Thunderbirds wasn't a spur-of-the-moment decision. I had lots of conversations with Mum and we both realised that this was one hell of an opportunity. This brand-new league was starting up, the timing seemed right, I wasn't studying and, ultimately, we both knew that playing with some of the best netballers in the world was only going to improve my game. The ANZ Championship, which was named after the main sponsor, ANZ Bank, was going to be good for me and good for my career. There really wasn't a downside to it. Adelaide had obviously seen me on the international scene and now I knew they wanted me, we began discussions about a contract. My first proper elite netball contract. There were five of us in the end, five

England players who accepted invitations to play in the world's first professional netball league: me, England vice-captain Karen Atkinson, Ama, Sonia and Tamsin Greenway. England Netball's director, Nigel Holl, saw the advantage of such an opportunity from the word go and he told the *Daily Express* that this move was only ever going to benefit English Netball, saying, 'It is a huge compliment to these English players and recognises the progress that the English game has made. When they return with advanced skills, training ideas and having experienced another level of domestic competition week in week out, their input will be crucial to the national squad.' All positive, right? You might wonder why I am putting this in but you will see how the attitudes changed over the next couple of years – and not only changed, but became so narrow-minded that my international career was put in jeopardy.

We worked out a deal for Raoul to fly over to do a six-month school exchange in Adelaide. Mum knew how much it would mean to me to have Raoul with me as I started playing for a brand-new team, in a brand-new league, living in a new country. So I did it; we made the move over. Mum had travelled to Adelaide in the late seventies and she remembered it having a similar feel to Bournemouth. She thought moving to a great rural city would be a good first step into Aussie life for me. I would live out there for five months of the year, a couple of months pre-season, and then three months of the actual season, before coming back to England. It was all quite exciting at the time; the main thing was that I got a salary, but also I could ask for things from the team and it would just happen. 'I need a car.' 'Yep, no problem!' This was a whole new way of life. I could make a career out of playing this sport now and it was pretty cool. I saw it as a natural progression for my netball game.

I signed a two-year contract and had a couple of amazing years in Adelaide. I rented a place in the suburb of Glenelg the first year and my boyfriend at the time, Luke Yeates, came over from England to stay. He was a sailing instructor and I had met him at the Southampton Boat Show, which Mum and I would always go along to as a birthday treat for me as it was held in September. My love of sailing always increased tenfold after these visits and this time I'd bought my Hobie Cat, a fifteen-foot sailing catamaran. Mum joked that as well as a boat I got an instructor as a package deal – I wasn't complaining! So Luke, Raoul and I lived a bit of a happy family existence for a while. It was pretty cool; I'd come home after training and cook dinner and we'd all eat together. They were such simple things but it meant a lot to me. I have always lived by myself or with family; I would never opt for a team house. You do get girls who rent a house with their teammates but I love having my own space and being able to come home and not have to talk about netball. It's OK not to live and breathe your sport – in fact, I think it's key to keeping you sane and letting your mind rest. Getting that work–life balance is essential, whether you are playing sport at an elite level or reaching your target in an office; you need to be able to come home and switch off. It is an important element of my game and it means I am able to go in fresh the next day. Your home is your domain and an area where you should be able to be comfortable and be at one with yourself.

It was nice to have an escape and I started making friends locally, not just in the netball circle, which was important too. I even joined a local sewing group when Mo'onia Gerrard and I saw an advert for a 'knit and natter' session after training one day. It was full of local pensioners who would put the world to rights while they knitted and we ended up going for several weeks. It was very therapeutic and inspirational listening to these women talk. Mum came out to visit too and stayed in my little apartment. She loved it, and I loved hosting her for a change!

In the netball league back in England I had had talks with England Netball about cementing the strong partnership Sonia and I had when we represented the country, and we decided it was a good idea for us to both sign for the same team. I had been with Team Bath for ten years now and we had won the Superleague three times, but it was time to move on. Sonia and I signed to Surrey Storm and we got paid £15 for each quarter we played. In that first season we came first in the league, which earned us a bonus of around £100 each. Hey, it was something! So that is how my life was looking: I would be in Australia for five months, playing for Thunderbirds for three of those, before returning to play for England and for Surrey Storm with Sonia when I was back home.

At the beginning of 2009 Sue Hawkins, a former national player for Australia, took over as England coach and in an interview with a sports website, she told a reporter that she considered Sonia and me to be the strongest aspect of the England team. We were known as the M&Ms and were a force to be reckoned with. 'We have the strongest combinations in defence of anywhere in the world with Sonia Mkoloma and Geva Mentor,' she said. 'England didn't perform to their highest level at the World Championships, you just have to look to the last quarter, that is something we have been addressing. As a team they will be really looking to step out every quarter and be on top every quarter.' I liked Sue straight away. She had a no-nonsense approach and she was getting the team focused on a part of the game that I knew was important – fighting until the very last second of a match. We had a very successful series with her against Jamaica at the start of 2009, winning the series 3–0, and coming from our one-goal defeat in the World Championships this really helped. We were ranked fourth in the world to Jamaica's third and it felt good to get that win under our belt.

In 2010 I signed a new three-year contract with Adelaide Thunderbirds and this was the year we went on to win the ANZ Championship, my first ever ANZ title. We had got close in 2008 and 2009 and then in 2010 we managed to earn ourselves a place in the grand final. Our home venue changed from the Priceline Stadium, with a seating capacity of 3,200, to the Adelaide Entertainment Centre, which had a seating capacity of over 11,000. The roar of the crowd was deafening and it made the whole final so thrilling, I didn't want it to end! We defeated the Waikato Bay of Plenty Magic side from New Zealand by ten goals and it was a great way to start my new-season signing. My first premiership title!

But 2010 was also to be my last year with Adelaide. The rules of the competition changed, perhaps because we'd won, and now the league would only allow one main import per team. We had signed a Jamaican player, Carla Borrego, as a new shooter earlier that year and the club chose her as their main import, which meant if I wanted to carry on playing for Thunderbirds I had to drop down and play in the league below.

I was initially shocked and then sad, whereas Mum was fuming when she found out what was happening and flew over to take part in one of the meetings. Basically, Thunderbirds still wanted me but they had offered the position to play in the ANZ league to Carla and I was dropped to play in the state league, the league below. I might get the opportunity to play with the top team but not compete with them – the team I had just won the championship with! When the realisation of it all set in, I was stunned. I had come over to play top netball, and I had been playing just that the last couple of years. I didn't want to take a step down. But I had already signed a new three-year contract and I didn't know what I could do. Mum certainly did though; she wasn't going to accept any bullshit and had a meeting with the head coach Jane Woodlands-Thompson and the CEO. She came out and told me straight that I had to get out. She took matters into her own hands and spoke to one of the other Australian teams in the ANZ Championship, the Vixens. The coach was none other than Julie Hoornweg, the England coach I had been guided by in the very beginning, and when Mum contacted her and explained the situation, her response was simple. 'We'll have Geva. Whatever happens, we'll have her.'

Julie told Mum that if the crap hit the fan, the Vixens would support me. And by that point, it was most definitely getting serious. Thunderbirds had threatened court action; they were going to sue me for breach of contract. But Mum and I organised our own management team and they argued that Thunderbirds too were in breach of contract. The contract I had signed stipulated that I should be playing in the ANZ Championship and not a state league, so they could take me to court but equally I could take them! They did indeed try. My managers, Allison Tranquilli, an ex-basketballer for Australia, and Mel Jones, who was an Australian cricketer, had set up a firm and were ready to fight my corner. Adelaide were putting a 'restraint of trade' defence against me, citing that I couldn't go and play for anyone else. But they were blown out of the water in the ensuing legal battle and I was released from my contract.

Mum had also approached Kate Palmer, the CEO of Netball Australia, to alert her to the situation and she was horrified. She was shocked at the way Thunderbirds were acting and she wanted me to find other imports to see if they were going through the same problems after the rule change. Netball Australia had no understanding of what was going on at some of these clubs. And in a nutshell, that is how I ended up going to Vixens.

It was a sad end to my time with Adelaide. Although that third year wasn't the smoothest with all the issues off court, winning, like I mentioned before, can mask a lot of cracks. Jane hadn't exactly been a supportive coach to me or a few of my teammates before we won the championship in 2010. In that season we had a few bad defeats and one that sparked everything off happened after we had a 'bye' week. The club had given us the weekend 'off' – no game was scheduled, plus we had the whole week before that weekend off too. It gave us the chance to have a bit of a break mentally and physically and it split up the season. After playing against West Coast Fever in Perth, four of us from the team decided to go to Bali. We thought a couple of days of massages and chilling out would be perfect, then we'd come back all refreshed and ready for training the next week and a game the week after. So we checked we were OK to do that, which we were, and we went across to Bali, which was just a three-hour flight from Perth. We had a great time; it was nice to chill out and relax with the girls.

What I didn't know at the time but have learned since is

that Bali is quite a party destination for Australians. Lots of Aussies go over there to get drunk and party. Yes, you can hire out villas and have a nice tranquil time – like we did! – but most of the time people would go out there to get drunk. I don't drink, and we spent our days on the beach getting massages and just chilling. It was a lovely, relaxing break that helped us recharge. We came back to a normal training week and then we flew up to Sydney for an away game.

Sydney Swifts had always been a bit of a nemesis for us – the Victoria and NSW interstate games were always quite intense – and on that day we got beaten badly. Admittedly we didn't play well as a team; it was one of those games where everyone was 'off', but it didn't help that Jane made a few odd coaching decisions. She moved a few people into different positions and we ended up getting beaten by ten or fifteen goals. That is a horrible loss in these championships. And the next day it was reported in the papers that the game had been lost due to 'The Bali Four'. The press had somehow decided we had been on a boozy trip to Bali and been distracted, and basically blamed the loss on the four of us who went away. 'The Bali Four' label came from an incident a couple of years before about a group of drug dealers who were sent to prison after a drugs bust and had been labelled 'The Bali Ten'. So for some reason, because we had lost a netball match, we were being likened to a gang of hardened criminals!

We were pulled apart by the media and Jane grilled us

one by one over our 'antics' in Bali. The whole ordeal was blown way out of proportion and was nasty. One of the girls who came with us was quite young and it really knocked her confidence. Whenever the team went out to take part in netball clinics or appearances, people assumed that we were doing community service. It was pretty incredible that all that was going on off court and yet we were still able to get our act together as a team and win the competition. But it wasn't just me (and the rest of us who went to Bali) who left the team after that. There was a mass exodus. I think Jane mishandled this incident but there's no doubting her success over the years. She is now in charge of the Women's Development Programme at Magpies, the team I am currently playing for and I will be professional and civil when I see her but I won't forget what happened.

It was my first taste of negative press. The problem I had was that the story was just complete crap; it just wasn't true. I could understand the negative story if we had done all or any of that but we hadn't and yet no one was listening to our side of the story. I was glad to be leaving Adelaide; it turned out to be the best move I would make. And while all this was going on in Australia, things weren't looking so good for me in the England camp either . . .

8 FROM THUNDERBIRD TO VIXEN AND BEYOND!

'The most dangerous phrase in the English language is: "We've always done it this way".'   Grace Hopper

You think you can only handle so much, you think there must be a limit to it. But then again, they do say it never rains but it pours, and I felt as if I was standing in a torrential downpour. While all that was happening with Adelaide, there were whisperings that all was not well in the England camp. Anna Mayes, who was the assistant national coach to head coach Sue Hawkins, wasn't happy about players playing in Australia and still representing England. When the England squad for the Commonwealth Games in Delhi, which was going to be held in October 2010, was announced, to say it was a closely fought selection would be an understatement. Anna didn't want me or Sonia on the team, not because of who we were but because of what we were doing. She didn't think we were showing commitment to England and she didn't see how playing in the ANZ in Australia, in this new dimension of professional sport, would serve my ability as a player for England. Her vision for the England team was that players playing out in New Zealand and Australia should not be part of it.

It was such a blinkered approach. Why should I not play in Australia, in the best league in the world, and also be part of the England team? She couldn't see that one would benefit the other and thought I should have to choose one or the other. But she was only assistant coach at the time, and my teammates made their feelings very clear. Sonia and I needed to be part of the squad at the Commonwealth Games, that was the overriding opinion in the team. 'They are the best defenders we have,' was their argument, 'we need them.' Sue Hawkins took their opinions on board and Sonia and I were selected but it was the start of something that was only going to escalate further. For now, though, we joined the girls and went to Delhi to get on with the job in hand.

This was my third Commonwealth Games and it was the first time that the Games had been held in India. Going to Delhi was an interesting experience; there was abject poverty and yet you'd also see majestic places like the Taj Mahal. There was a bit of controversy over the fact that the athletes' village hadn't been finished and the rooms weren't quite ready for us – little things like the light sockets weren't installed properly and some walls hadn't been painted. And the plumbing was a little dubious; I think one of the netball rooms had a blocked toilet, which is never a good thing when you have a lot of athletes wanting to use it (those nerves often get the better of us!) But apart from that, I loved every minute. Team England had two apartment blocks and England Netball were across two floors of one of them. We had the women's and men's hockey team on our floors, which was cool. Meeting up with familiar faces and people from other countries from past Games gave us a sense of ease and familiarity. As always, the food halls and the games room were enjoyable places to hang out; it was where you'd find lots of athletes chilling, mingling, switching off and having fun. Kit-swapping had become a big thing and during the first week you walk around and check out the different countries and see what kit they're wearing, see what you like the look of. Canada normally have the best garments; they have really nice hoodies and T-shirts. And then in the second week you swap and exchange kit if you want, although you have to be good at haggling! 'I'll give you my T-shirt if you give me your hoodie,' that sort of thing. It's a great way to get mementoes from each tournament and it's all a bit of fun. I was never up for it, I was too precious about the kit I had, even if it didn't fit or it wasn't the greatest. But I always liked going around with the girls who would be swapping. It was hilarious to watch, this bartering between nations over a T-shirt! The only kit I suppose I ever thought I should get was something from the St Lucia team, something from my dad's home country. In my most recent Games on the Gold

Coast I finally swapped something and managed to get some shorts from St Lucia. I was super-chuffed about that.

It's good to see the same athletes each Games. In the team sports especially, which don't have the same turnover as individual sports, you often get to meet up again with the same people. We became quite close to the hockey lot and the basketball team. And then you'd end up following them in the competition and throughout the year to see how they were getting on. There were a couple of boxers I first met in Manchester who we got quite friendly with: Paul Smith and, at the following Games, his younger brother, Steve, and then at these Games in Delhi, another brother, Callum Smith. That was pretty cool; what a family!

We got through our group stages with ease, beating South Africa, Barbados, the Cook Islands and Papua New Guinea before losing to New Zealand to come second in our group. We then faced Australia in the semi-finals and lost 45–51. Sonia and I were part of the starting seven now; we were number one and number two in the defensive unit and we did our jobs. We were quite an intimidating duo to the opposition and that is why our teammates wanted us in the team – they knew we would cause trouble for the shooters. But in the last quarter they took me off. It was a bizarre decision as I am the sort of player who grinds down the opposition. I come into play in those last crucial moments. This match felt like I was getting my mojo, I was starting to read play, get my hand to the ball, get the intercepts, and it felt like everything was slowing down around me and I could predict the ball's movement. I really felt like I was getting into my rhythm – and then Anna decided to take me off. I was surprised, but beyond that I didn't think anything of it. I think I just thought OK, that decision has been made for good reason, it was obviously the best thing for the team at the time. And then Australia just took over and they rolled us. It was bitterly disappointing; we thought we had that match from the starting whistle. It wasn't until after the game, when a few people said to me, 'Why did they take you off?', that I started to question the decision. Mum said it too. She wasn't happy about it; she knew my style, she knew the final quarter is where I come good, I fight it out. So I guess it started to weigh on my mind and I started to question it. We ended up facing Jamaica in the bronze medal play-off again, but this time we didn't buckle under pressure. We went out and fought for bronze and ended up winning quite comfortably (70–47) against what had always been our 'bogie team'.

When I flew back to Australia at the end of 2010, I wasn't an Adelaide Thunderbird any more, I was with the Melbourne Vixens. I was lucky that the coach was Julie Hoornweg, my first England coach, who'd scouted me all those years ago. We met up a couple of times to chat as she wanted to check I was OK after everything that had happened with Adelaide. She had given me her support as soon as the trouble began and I was grateful, but I knew she wouldn't want to put me on the team without scoping me out first. She hadn't seen me play for a while so I did some training with the team and she liked what she saw. I moved to Melbourne at the beginning of 2011 and started the new year with a new team.

The Vixens already had a goalkeeper, Bianca Chatfield, and a goal defender, Julie Corletto, who were both in the Australian Diamonds set-up. It didn't put me in the best position when I joined; it wasn't like the club needed strong defenders when the two already on the team were playing for the Diamonds! This probably got back to Anna in England too. But I couldn't think about that now. I had a new club to focus on. Julie put me in the team as wing defence. Yes, you heard right, wing defence. I am sure there are a couple of photos of me out there playing with a WD on my dress! I had one practice game as a wing defence, which I remember very clearly. We were playing in Bendigo, a regional town in Victoria, and they had me start as WD, Julie as GD and Bianca as GK. I don't think I made it to the end of that first quarter before the coach called 'time' and moved Bianca to GD and Julie to WD and me back to goalkeeper. And from that game onwards we never looked back. I managed to hold down the GK bib, Julie played a very good WD and Bianca started to solidify her position as GD. I felt a bit bad; basically I had come in and pushed these girls out of their normal positions to make way for me! But in doing so they have then excelled at their new posts and everything has just worked. And it's worked a bloody sight better than having me as WD! I think I spent my time running around like a headless chicken. Wing attacks are so speedy and, although I could just about get away with using my arms and my reaching range, trying to keep up with these girls was just . . . well, I was a fish out of water, that's for sure. I felt a lot more at home when I put the GK bib back on.

The situation with England Netball still wasn't great. I just couldn't see the reasoning as to why they weren't happy with what I was doing. I've forgotten that period – I must have blanked it from my memory. It was an emotional time. I was also struggling with a herniated disc in my back that was pushing on my sciatic nerve. It felt like a knife was running all up and down my hamstring, into my calf and then back up again. I had it all throughout the Com Games in Delhi but with the right treatment and medication I managed to get through the matches.

I went on an antidepressant drug because it was meant to be good for nerves, I had two epidurals, I had a nerve root sleeve injection, which is where they put a needle near where the nerve leaves the spine and then inject a long-acting steroid and a long-acting anaesthetic into it. I looked a little bit like the penguin Mumble in *Happy Feet* when he returns to his family with the antennae in his back. But nothing really touched it and so I just got on with it and, over time, it just sort of cleared itself up. Well, I could perhaps put it down to something – or someone – else but more on that later.

I was back in the squad for the 2011 World Netball Championships in Singapore, although things between Anna and me still weren't great. I felt I was getting the blame for the fact that English netball players had been given this opportunity! I remember saying in a BBC interview after the competition that it would be beneficial for the England squad if more home-grown players joined me in the ANZ league. I was quoted as saying, 'Obviously England need to step it up, so if we get more English girls playing over here and strengthen our Superleague in the UK too that would help. The ANZ league is the top domestic competition that I can play in so I will really improve my netball.' It probably didn't help the situation but it was true; I didn't want anyone to be scared of girls going out to hone their skills and then using those skills wearing an England dress. Sue Hawkins was still the coach and the team were feeling confident, Sonia and I were confident in our defensive unit and the whole team had an air of expectation about them. We wanted to get better than a bronze; we wanted to show everyone what we were capable of. The pool matches, usually a chance for the starting seven to do a couple of quarters and then fresh legs to take over, allowing us to stay rested for the next stages, were completely crazy. We had two young defenders in the squad that competition, Eboni Beckford-Chambers and Stacey Francis, and then Sonia and me as the two experienced defenders. But instead of playing Sonia and me together for half a match, getting us used to playing together, they played us in different combinations; they had me playing with Stacey and Sonia playing with Eboni. It really bothered me. Why wasn't I being given any match practice with Sonia, the starting GD? It was so frustrating. It felt like we didn't get any quarters together at all. And then I started overthinking and stressing myself out: what if I'm not the starting GK any more? I would have to work harder. But then if I AM the starting GK, I don't feel like I have been given enough time to gel again with Sonia. All these little niggles started getting to me and it's the last thing you need in a tournament because it's a complete waste of energy. And in the end, after playing all the lead-up games in different combinations, we then faced New Zealand in the semi-finals and Sonia and I were back together in the starting seven. I was like, 'What the hell?!' What was the point of all that mixing?! By then we hadn't played together for months, we hadn't had a build-up together in this tournament and now you are expecting us to click for the semi-final? It was terrible coaching if you ask me. Sonia and I were good enough players to make it work – we had had years together and we knew each other well – but we still lost, and I don't necessarily think it was from the defensive end. The coaching wasn't great, the atmosphere wasn't great, the environment wasn't great. I got a cold sore because of the stress and ended up with a massive fat lip because I tried to treat it with medication. The last couple of games everyone was asking me if I was all right as it looked like I had been punched in the mouth! It was turning out to be the worst tournament ever. We ended up playing Jamaica again in the bronze-medal play-offs and I was so wound up inside by everything at that point. I was fired up and I wanted to win. I wasn't going to let this bronze medal go; this competition had to be good for something! I was on a mission. I remember saying to Sonia, 'Right, let's just get this done.' In my mind no one was going to get in the way and we ended up winning fairly easily. I remember standing on the podium after collecting our medals and everyone was obviously so excited and I was just numb. Why were we happy with bronze again? Why weren't we fighting? We had a team that was good enough to really make a mark on the championship, and I felt that with a different approach we could have challenged for a better medal.

Yes, we came away with something but I had this dissatisfied taste in my mouth. It felt like a waste. The new girls on the squad were happy with a medal but I knew deep down that we were better than that. I had this real yearning for a better medal and it felt like a chance had been wasted. I did make sure I didn't just think this; I wanted to talk about it afterwards with the coaches so they understood why I didn't think we were strategically sound. In the debrief after the semi-finals, I said just that: 'You can't expect a starting seven combination to fire in the finals if you don't give it a chance in the early rounds. It just won't work.'

Now, you see that happen in all the top competitions. You may not be on together for the full game or even half the game but at least you have your starting seven on for a quarter or two throughout the different games or pool matches. That bronze medal match, on 10 July 2011, was to be my last England game for over fourteen months.

Anna Mayes took over from Maggie Jackson, who had taken over from Sue Hawkins as head coach after the World Championships. Maggie had stepped in when Sue had to resign for personal reasons. Now Anna was taking over from Maggie and I was being punished for wanting to improve my netball game in another country. I had been officially dropped from the England team.

9 NO LONGER A ROSE

'How dare they?! They are national selectors. It is their job to make decisions and not sit on the sodding fence!'

Yvonne Mentor

NETBALL works on a four-year cycle. You have the Commonwealth Games in the third year, the World Championships the following year (year four) and the two years prior are spent preparing again for those big tournaments in a series of test matches. At the end of July 2011 I had no idea that I wouldn't be putting on an England dress for nearly a year and a half.

I was back in Melbourne in August and preparing for my second season with the Vixens. It was good exposure being in Melbourne. They love their netball. Adelaide is a small city but living in Victoria and playing for a Melbourne team meant I was exposed to a lot more opportunities. We went out into the community and I developed a real love of coaching and working with youngsters and kids across the multicultural spectrum. It was similar to my early days on the England team when we had the Sporting Champions programme. I loved chatting to the kids and meeting lots of different people, making appearances at lots of different venues. I formed some partnerships with Netball Australia and I used my profile of playing with Melbourne Vixens to be able to actually get out in the community. I was able to explore and be involved in another side of netball.

Mum and Raoul joined me for Christmas in 2011. I had a little place in Melbourne and Mum wanted to be around at the start of 2012 for the Aussie Open tennis tournament, which was being held in Olympic Boulevard, Melbourne Park. I think she was also a little worried about me; she knew that things weren't great with England Netball and I was still finding my feet a bit with Vixens, so she flew out to see me. When I joined Vixens I became good friends with some of the players from the Melbourne Tigers, the basketball team. I remember one evening, in those dull days between Christmas and New Year, I convinced Raoul to come out for the evening to just 'hang out' with these guys. Raoul liked playing a bit of basketball so I thought it would be good for him. I suppose I was a bit of a chaperone. I wasn't dressed up, I was just hanging out with my brother; I didn't need to doll myself up. And that is when I met my future husband, Lachlan. He was out with some of his cricket buddies and we got chatting by the bar. I was in a T-shirt and jeans and felt a bit of a scruff but there is no way I could have predicted I would meet a guy that I would get on so well with on a relaxed night out with my brother. We hit it off and at the end of the night we exchanged numbers.

Our first proper date was at a rooftop cinema. We had planned to meet on the corner of Bourke and Swan Streets, a busy spot in Melbourne, a big intersection with lots of foot traffic because the Bourke Street mall and shops begin there. Not only was I not sure what corner he would be on, I wasn't sure if I would recognise him or not! I wasn't paying much attention to his looks the night we met, I just remembered him being tall. Luckily, we found each other – well, he found me. I'd been smiling at all the tall men who walked past just in case! The date went well. We started by having a drink at a bar and a couple of people came up to me to ask if I was a tennis player, probably because the Aussie Open was about to start. I think Lachy liked this, the fact that I stood out and appeared to be 'somebody'. We then moved to the rooftop of the bar and watched a movie under the night sky. That bit was romantic, even though the film wasn't – *Trainspotting*. I didn't mind. It was a classic, even though probably not ideal for a first date!

The next day Mum, Raoul and I were meant to be going to the Aussie Open, and I'd said to Lachy on our date, 'If you want to come down tomorrow you're welcome to.' And indeed he did. He ended up meeting Mum the day after we had our first date and Mum, bless her, who bloody loves tennis, gave up her seat for the men's doubles match so he could sit with me. But she could see the sparks, she said.

She was happy for me if I liked him, and at first there wasn't much not to like. I won't lie, I was flattered by his attention. He was tall, he was handsome and charming and when you spend so much time working, training and playing with women you don't always get much chance to meet men. Especially outside of the netball world. We had similar interests in sports and we got on well and it was nice that Raoul and Mum got to meet him before she went back to the UK. So I started my 2012 season with Vixens with a new boyfriend and it was at that point that I decided to stay out in Australia permanently. Lachy's mum had a vacant apartment in Melbourne as she was mostly based in another city, Geelong, so as it came to the end of my season and everything was going well between us, I ended up moving in with him. It was the next stage of our relationship.

After the ANZ season finished in July, I was due to start a new job that had been organised with the Vixens in August. Back in April I had been invited to attend the trials for England, which would be happening in July and would decide the squad for the next nine months. I rang Mum in a bit of a panic. I wanted to be at trials but I knew I couldn't commit to the first test series with the team in Jamaica in September as I would be working. Mum told me that she didn't bring any of her children up to not be upfront and honest and simply said, 'Geva, just tell them you have too much stuff happening in Oz, you won't be available for the Jamaica series but you would be available for all other England commitments.' So I rang England Netball and explained the situation – that I was so eager to go for trials but I wouldn't be available for the test series in Jamaica. I even asked them if they still wanted me to come for the selection process, knowing I wouldn't be available for one test. They told me on that call that they understood and yes, they still wanted me to try out. I made a point of checking that they understood my decision and I got them to confirm I was still requested for trials, as I pay for my own flights back to the UK and they aren't cheap! Having that confirmation meant it wasn't going to be a wasted trip, I thought, and I flew back to the UK after the season with Vixens finished and attended the trials at Hatfield.

At the end of the first weekend I was called into an office and there were six people all sitting round a table. There was the selection panel, which included Colette Thomson (the coach who saw me at my very first under-seventeen try-outs) and Anna Mayes. Colette was also the assistant coach for England and I know that this next moment was a professional decision and I'm sure nothing personal. They asked me if I would make myself available for the Jamaica series in September. I again explained that this wasn't possible and that I had already spoken to people at England Netball about it and had it confirmed that it wasn't a problem. But they decided to put it to a vote: if I couldn't make myself available for the whole of the season – including Jamaica, Australia, New Zealand and then the series in Australia again – I wasn't going to make the squad. My stomach just dropped. I remember that feeling to this day.

I have to be honest, I think the majority of people on the selection panel were in favour of me being selected, but then Colette Thomson spoke. She couldn't agree to it. She was from the old-school brigade I guess, the one that says you have to do it exactly this way, the right way. No ifs, no buts. And I wasn't doing it the right way and so it was a no. There was no compromise, no leeway. I was looking at her thinking, 'Who are you to have this totally black and white opinion and sway everyone else in this room?' I thought I had built up a really good relationship with Colette as she was one of my coaches when I played under-seventeens and assistant coach when I was in the under-twenty-ones. She knew how much playing for England meant to me. As I said, she is still involved with the team and I am of course respectful to her and professional. To her, it wasn't an emotional decision, it was a case of applying the standards she believed in. And while I respect that, it was hard to take. I don't think I'll ever forget her decision. So it went to a vote and in the end two selectors sided with me and said yes, while Colette and another selector said no. Two selectors abstained from the vote, which meant the final decision went to Anna. She told me that she had to set an example and that her decision was no. I wasn't going to be on the team for the next year.

I was in floods of tears when I spoke to Mum later that evening. I was so frustrated and cross with myself. I thought I should have just lied, not mentioned I wouldn't be available and then just pulled a sicky before the Jamaica series and said I was too ill to fly. But I knew deep down that wasn't the answer. I was honest and it cost me my place on the team.

Mum was absolutely livid about the vote. Not about Colette or Anna or the selectors who voted, but the ones who abstained. 'How dare they?!' she shouted. 'They are national selectors. It is their job to make decisions and not sit on the sodding fence!'

I have no memory of what happened to England in the Jamaica series; I was still so hurt and, sadly, I probably didn't care. I flew back heartbroken to Melbourne, to my flat, to Lachy, to Vixens. In October, England flew out to Australia and then New Zealand to compete in a seven-week test series. I decided that the only way to prove my passion for England was to open the lines of communication. It was a bit like being back on the bench again; I could still help the team and give advice even if I wasn't playing.

I found out that some of their practice sessions were being held on courts that had a very hard playing surface (they should be sprung), which could lead to injuries due to the impact. I rang England Netball and suggested other venues. It was really tough, though: I was literally just round the corner from where the first test was being held and I was at home twiddling my thumbs. I was sending messages, pacing around the living room, and just wanted to scream, 'Use me!' I was fit, I'd been training, I was there, I was ready! But instead they flew out a new player from the UK. I haven't heard of her since but that didn't stop it hurting at the time. I couldn't understand why they would fly a less experienced girl halfway round the world to play in a position that I could play and was more experienced at playing than her. But I kept making contact, I sent more messages, I kept trying to keep the lines of communication open and positive. For example, I remember mentioning to Anna that as I had been playing against a lot of the Diamonds for the past four years I knew them pretty well and I could perhaps provide information that would help her and the coaching team.

When the team flew to New Zealand for that leg of the series, Pam Cookey, the goal shooter, was allowed to fly home as she had work commitments. Netball isn't a professional sport in the UK like it is in Australia, and all the girls playing in the league in England also have full- or part-time jobs.

That was it. I couldn't believe it. Talk about double standards. Mum now gives this example to all the parents she meets. She has very little faith in England Netball and she will never forgive them for the way they treated me. She tells all the parents to focus on putting their daughters' best interests first and to question everything they are told by England Netball. I was actually quite naive about a lot of this at the time, although I like to think that things have improved nowadays. You can see why Mum is so passionate about it; she only had my welfare in mind and hated to see me being treated unfairly.

When Australia went over to the UK at the start of 2013,

they lost the three-match test series 3–0. This was a great result for England – the ten-time world champions beaten at Wembley. The mood was one of pure celebration and some of the players were backflipping down the court. It was a wake-up call for Australia not to underestimate England, but it was obvious to those in the netball world that Australia hadn't taken over their strongest side. One of the reasons was that this tour takes place in the Australia off-season, so a lot of the girls were being rested or weren't quite match-fit. I don't think Australia will make that mistake again.

I was really happy for the girls winning so comfortably. At the end of the day, if Australia want to bring an under-strength side to face England so be it. England can only play who the Aussies put out and it was a tremendous boost to the team knowing that we could beat a team of Australians 3–0. I think my only concern was that we had the potential to get carried away and complacent. I knew it wouldn't always be that easy, I knew there were some big guns they didn't play, and those big guns brought with them a lot of experience. I rang Anna and congratulated her and the team. All the time I was trying to show enthusiasm; I didn't want to be forgotten or cast aside. I was determined to show Anna that even though I wasn't playing, I was still hungry for that England dress. It still meant so much to me. And I knew I had so much to give my country. And the talking and the constant communicating and messaging must have helped. Eventually I found myself sitting down with the selection panel again. They could see that this was obviously something that I wanted to keep doing. I wanted to play in Australia to improve my game and they slowly started to see the benefits and finally started making it work. Suddenly we were talking about planning schedules and when I would be flying back and how it could work with me living and playing in Oz. Timing-wise, I guess I was quite lucky. Throughout this period I had never missed a big tournament; I hadn't missed the Commonwealth Games or the World Championships. And I never gave up on England. I never accepted that being dropped was the end. That would have been easy. I could have just stayed with Vixens and enjoyed a career in Australia without worrying about playing for England ever again. But I wasn't ready to not be a Rose – I wanted to see England in that number-one spot.

All this time I hadn't been playing with England I was enjoying my time with the Vixens. It gave me a real purpose and it was great for the team when we made the final at the end of the season in 2013. We ended up losing to Waikato Bay of Plenty Magic, which was hard, but quite a talking point in the championship as it was the first time a New Zealand side had ever won the ANZ.

My first game back in the England squad was on 25 September 2013. Exactly 450 days since I had been banned. I was picked to play in a test series against South Africa that was being held at Wembley. England Netball didn't make a song and dance about my being absent and then suddenly back in the squad, although a few commentators picked up on my return to court. We always play three matches in a test series but I didn't get to play in the first or make the starting seven in the second. I came on in the third or fourth quarter of that match. In the third match I was a starter and I have pretty much stayed in that position ever since. So was the first-match snub to teach me a lesson? Was putting me on late in the game in the second match to spite me? Was the underlying message, 'Look, Geva, you can't just waltz back on to court straight away like nothing has happened'? OK, I could cope with that. Seeing Anna again and being back in the squad wasn't weird. I never had anything personal against her, I just found her approach so narrow-minded. We have always had a pretty good relationship and while I was banned I was always trying to keep in contact and so when I eventually came back on the team, it wasn't this massive thing. I'd been absent from playing but I hadn't let them forget me, and so there was no bad blood. I was pleased to be able to show how much I could contribute to the team on court as well as off it. My biggest bugbear over the whole thing revolved around Colette being there. She didn't have the final say but she had the biggest impact.

Coming back into the squad and being back among the girls again was bloody brilliant. I was back with players I'd known since a young age – having laughs, having jokes, striving towards the same goal, which was all I wanted. The girls were intrigued about what it was like playing out in Australia, especially the media aspect of the game. All the games in ANZ are televised as netball is such a big sport out there and the girls wanted to know what it was like, being part of netball when it had such elevated status. The Australian leagues were the pinnacle of netball and, after I came back, a lot of the English girls started aspiring to get contracts out in Australia and New Zealand. That wasn't the big deal now that it had been and I had made it possible. It wasn't easy for me to stick to my guns and not come running back to the English league as soon as the mood changed in the England camp, but I kept focused on what was best for my game. I could have easily relented and come back to play for an English club, but would my netball improve? Doubtful. Would it have been of any benefit? Probably not. I am pleased it has worked out the way it has. It's nice for girls to be able, if they have that opportunity, to go out and play in the Australian league, the premier league for netball in the world. To know that if they get an offer from an Australian side, they can accept it without fear of consequence. They know that if they are good enough, they can still represent their country. The important point is, they have a choice. I have been called a trailblazer and a pioneer but, to be honest, I am just glad others are able to have that opportunity.

Life was good in Melbourne. Things with Lachy were going OK. He would often come to games at the weekend if it didn't clash with his cricket matches. The Vixens were building momentum in the 2014 season. Bianca Chatfield and I were forming a good connection as GK and GD and we made it into the final that season. We didn't want a repeat of the previous season and on 22 June we ended up beating the Queensland Firebirds to win the title. It was the second time Vixens had won the premiership, but the first time was long before I joined the team and I was so pleased to be involved in this second victory. No, forget that – I was elated! I left Melbourne for England on a high, knowing that I wanted to achieve the same result with England in this year's Commonwealth Games. I was fed up with bronze, I wanted a different colour!

Lachy had managed to get permission from the school where he was a PE teacher to come over for the Games, which were being held in Glasgow that year. It was good to have him there. It would be the first time he would see me play at a major tournament and he had been with me when the England ban was in place, so he knew how much it meant to me. Mum, Raoul and lots of my friends and family had travelled up too and I was excited to share the experience of a major tournament with everyone.

I felt the England team had a real chance this year. Playing in Australia had done exactly what I wanted it to do; we as players didn't put the Silver Ferns and Diamonds on pedestals any more. I had been playing with them and against them week in and week out and I had learned from them and gained confidence. And I knew now that they were human, after all; they had strengths and weaknesses just like us. I was more battle-hardened too. I was ready to fight! The BBC wanted to hear my thoughts on our chances and I remember being really upbeat and positive and saying: 'We have been talking the talk for many years but now I'd like to think this is the year we can walk the walk and show the world what England are all about.'

This was my fourth Games and it never loses its excitement. The athletes walking around the village, the likes of Usain Bolt and people like that giving the place an extra vibe. Team England were buzzing. I felt like we were in good form and I personally felt in good form. We had lost Pam Cookey due to an anterior cruciate ligament injury and we had a couple of debuts in the team, but we felt OK about the balance. We pottered along throughout the tournament, changed a few combinations and kept things nice and fresh.

We went up against Australia in our final Group B match and we came out fighting. We were fired up, we were ready, we knew we could compete against the top teams and now it was time to show it. The game against Australia was goal-for-goal and I think we had the momentum throughout. Australia made some changes and mixed up some of the positions to mess with us mentally. There was one girl who normally plays GK or GD and they put her in at WD to hound Serena Guthrie, who was WA for us. It was obvious their coach had told her to come in and bulldoze Serena; she had no intention of going for the ball, it was just about roughing up Serena and getting in her face. Losing to Australia hurt. We were 100 per cent in that game but then in the last few seconds Jo Harten's missed shot, the shot that would have won it for us, just came back down and the Diamonds went on to score, and won 49–48. We just couldn't finish it. Player errors and coaching decisions were to blame. And it made us more determined than ever to hit hard against New Zealand, who we were facing next in the semi-final.

The night before that match Anna insisted that we all make an appearance on the BBC's Commonwealth Games show. She wanted the whole team to go and do our bit of netball PR. It was going to be a very late night for the whole team and we'd probably only get a couple of minutes of airtime and, to be honest, I was dead against it. Eboni and I made our objections and said we didn't think it was appropriate for the team, who were playing in an important match the next day, to be up all night filming a BBC show. It shouldn't be how we prepared for a big match, the team should be rested and ready, we argued, but we were overruled.

The game was tough. We were matching the Silver Ferns goal for goal and you could probably say that the momentum was in England's favour for the majority of the game. In the final quarter two things happened that I thought altered our flow. Our GD, who had been on all game, was changed in the last five minutes. It was a weird decision. Not that the replacement was bad but when you have someone who has been grinding down the GA from the starting whistle and was dominating that circle, taking nine or ten rebounds and hustling the shooters, replacing her in the dying moments with someone who hadn't built up that 'presence' seemed like a very odd decision to me.

The score was level right up until the last seconds of the game and it was our centre pass. We took the ball, we moved it around court, we sent it into our goal third so our shooters were ready. And then just outside the circle, Kadeen Corbin, who was playing goal shooter, threw the ball away. She made a bad pass and threw it – quite literally – straight into the Silver Ferns centre. There was barely twenty seconds left to play and then all of a sudden the ball was whizzing down to us and they scored. They had won 35–34 in those final few seconds. We had lost. We had thrown away our chance to play for a gold medal. It was a wasted chance. We didn't need to tell ourselves that it was a glorious failure and that we had given as good as we got. We were better and we knew it; we just didn't seem to have it in us to prove it.

Everyone was distraught. This was my fourth Games and this defeat really hurt. Corbin was inconsolable. I went up to her at the end. She was in tears and she obviously felt completely to blame. She was crying and I started to well up too, but I put my arm round her to show her that we were a team. It shouldn't come down to those single moments. We have all had those 'one moments' in a sixty-minute game where we should have thrown a better pass or we should have got this ball or made that interception. But her tears were for the fact her mistake occurred in that last thirty seconds when we should have scored and won. That was really tough for her, and us.

Which led us into the Jamaica game. Yes, we were going to face Jamaica in the bronze medal play-off AGAIN. I'd like to say that losing by so little to New Zealand and Australia before that spurred us on to not leave the Games empty-handed but we didn't have any fight left. We were broken by this point; we'd had our hearts ripped to pieces against Australia and then ripped out losing to New Zealand, and when it came to the Jamaica game, we literally got rolled by them. They came into that match aggressive, fired up and ready and we were still hurting and deflated mentally. Everything we tried wasn't working, the umpiring wasn't the greatest, the combinations we had practised over and over weren't working. Mum walked out at half-time; she couldn't watch any more. We ended up losing by over ten goals. I had a black eye and fat lip after the match because the Jamaican goal shooter was swinging her elbows around every time she got the ball and I got too close and bore the brunt of it. It looked like I had been in a rugby game! When it was all over, Mum came to give me a hug. There were no words spoken between us, I just let her safe arms envelop me while I sobbed.

It was a horrible way to end the Games, the Games that we had hoped would be ours. We all went to the warm-down court afterwards and just sat there in silence. In utter dejection. We were all thinking the same thing, that this was going to take us a while to get over. This one really hurt. There is a convention in these competitions for our coach and management team to want us to remain behind and watch the final. It was torture. None of us wanted to watch the gold medal match knowing it should have been us on court. It seemed very unfair making us come out and sit among everybody to watch that game. We had to sit through the medal ceremony too. It left a really nasty taste at the end of our Commonwealth Games campaign, which had been ours for the taking. We had the team, we had the game plan . . . it was just horrible. I knew we wouldn't be looking ahead to the 2018 Com Games just yet. We were too busy licking our wounds.

10 WHAT DOESN'T BREAK YOU . . .

'It's OK if you fall down and lose your spark. Just make sure that when you get back up, you rise as the whole damn fire.'
Colette Werden

THE defeat at the Commonwealth Games was made slightly more palatable by going on holiday with Lachy for my thirtieth birthday in September. It was a holiday I had organised myself, which I normally did, and we went to Croatia and then Lanzarote. Unbeknown to me, Lanzarote was where he had planned on proposing and he told me afterwards, after he had done the deed, that he'd been walking around all day with the ring in his pocket but there were lots of rowdy people and it wasn't appropriate. In the end he proposed that evening, on our hotel balcony. I was due to have a big birthday party when we got back to Melbourne but he told me he had arranged it all with his mum to turn it into an engagement party instead. I had never really had a birthday party as I've always been travelling or playing – I never got to properly celebrate my eighteenth or twenty-first. So I thought I would really go to town for my thirtieth and booked a venue and entertainment . . . but it wasn't to be. It got turned into an engagement party and I just accepted that and laughed it off. If you are happy in a relationship, if you are with the man you want to spend the rest of your life with, this sort of thing might not matter. I think that's when my doubts first started, which was ironic as I now had a ring on my finger and, if anything, this was the thing I should have been the most sure about.

What I do know is that we got married on 20 December 2015, in Torquay, Victoria, Australia and we are now legally divorced, as of 5 November 2018. The relationship started off OK; I met him at a time in my life when I wanted a significant other to share it with. So I think when I met him, it was a bit of a relief; I had found someone, I was going to be all right.

Sonia, my English teammate who I had known for years and knew me better than most people, was my maid of honour and my two half-sisters, Inez and Noor, who came over from the Netherlands, were my flower girls. As a nice gesture I asked Lachy's sister Rachel to be a bridesmaid too. I had thought that he would ask Raoul to be in his groom's party but he didn't ask him so I had my brother in my bridal party as well. I had quite an entourage and he had a couple of his mates. Everything had already been organised for the wedding to take place in Australia and that was down to his parents. I'd wanted to get married in Hawaii or somewhere; I think I felt it should be a halfway point that both families could get to. But I was happy to go with the flow and convince mine to come to Australia. After all, I had been trying to get my dad over to this side of the world for years. Mum and many members of my family were there. I knew they'd spent a lot of money on flights and accommodation to come to the wedding for me and I think I felt a little guilty, as I was having serious doubts.

It wasn't a massive wedding; we had about eighty guests in total, and I wanted it to be laid-back and relaxed, so we had it on a nice golf course by the beach. We had an evening of canapés – I didn't want a poncy three-course set meal, I just wanted people to enjoy the scenery and for it to be casual. Dad gave me away and I was absolutely bawling my eyes out when I walked down the aisle. We had had a rehearsal the day before and the weather had been blisteringly hot, over forty degrees. Lachy couldn't make the rehearsal because he was due to play in a cricket match, although it ended up being cancelled due to the heat.

The wedding day itself was really emotional. We had planned to have the ceremony outside originally, but only an hour or so beforehand, the weather turned and there was a storm with gale-force winds and torrential rain! Everything had to be moved indoors and Lachy and everyone else who was there, a few friends and family who'd turned up early including some dear friends of ours, the

Caldwell family, just knuckled down to help and got everything inside and set up. I was so grateful to them all. So I walked down the aisle with my dad. I was emotional as I felt a bit out of control, given the weather, but there wasn't anything I could do so I had to let that go. And I was emotional because of the day. I don't normally display my emotions so openly but I was properly crying as Dad and I made our way down the aisle. And when I got to Lachy, I think I sort of hoped he would be emotional too. Look a little teary-eyed or something. But there was nothing. When someone I love is upset I know I always start to well up a bit just because they are crying, but from him there was nothing. OK, I thought, some men just don't show emotions, I get that.

Emotionless he might have been but he was also a very intelligent man, so I never felt I was ever going to win an argument because he always had all the answers. I like to stick to my guns if what I believe in is true and fair, and I can be stubborn about it, and he wouldn't ever give up or back down, so there was no point in us going to battle. It wasn't pleasant and I'm not a great one for confrontation; I just want to solve things and move on. And if things in our relationship weren't great before the wedding, they definitely weren't great after the wedding. Everyone says that the best bit of your relationship is the honeymoon period but it wasn't for me. Being on the road, travelling with netball, does take a lot of commitment and a lot of your time and you need to be with someone who not only understands but appreciates this. I guess we didn't really have the quality time together we needed before we got married to see if we were suited. The thing that baffles me is that he knew I was a netballer, he knew the commitments and sacrifices that had to be made to play this sport at the elite level, but he seemed to want someone who was going to be around when he got back from work, a wife first and foremost.

He also couldn't get his head round the fact that it wasn't going to be for ever, that I wasn't going to be playing at this level for the rest of my life. I was constantly telling him and reassuring him that in years to come I would be able to spend more time with him, more time at home. I ended up feeling very guilty for being a netballer.

To begin with, I think he was a bit swept away having a girlfriend who was in the public eye. Remember how big netball is in Australia. He has enjoyed being part of my netballing life in that sense, coming along to the nice events, doing the nice things. It was the little, everyday things that added up and chipped away at me. There were so many little things that I thought he did because they were best for our relationship, but perhaps I was just naive.

The biggest indicator, the big red flag for me that our marriage was never going to work, was the fact he didn't seem to understand my relationship with my mum and my brother. Mum and Raoul are massively important to me; the relationship I have with them is like no other and it is stronger than any other relationship I will ever have. So the fact that Lachy seemed not only not to like them but that it felt to me that he showed them so little respect, was what got to me the most. I understand that not all husbands have to like their mother-in-law or brother- or sisters-in-law and that's OK. It wasn't like they were living next door to us either; we were on the other side of the world for heaven's sake!

There is a good reason for me including all of this and it's not to air my dirty laundry in public or make you feel sorry for me. I know, too, that there are always two sides to every story and that Lachy has his good qualities. And it doesn't matter what people see for sixty minutes on a netball court – a fearless, confident, dominating goal-keeper, perhaps. I never let my personal life affect my netball but it would probably have come as a bit of a shock to those who know 'me on court' to see the other me. The one whose confidence was low, who was struggling, who wasn't sure where this relationship was headed. I was lucky I had netball to concentrate on. If I am totally honest I have tried to blank a lot of what happened from my mind. So I've asked Mum to contribute to this bit. She saw everything from a mum's point of view, of course, and is biased, but hopefully it will give you a good idea of the emotions I was dealing with.

'*Geva was hitting thirty and wanted someone to build a life with, start a family with . . . Because of her sport and her lifestyle, she wasn't meeting guys. Lachy was the only one who really showed any interest. A lot of guys were intimidated by her; they didn't feel they could approach her. Patrick Lucas, her PE teacher, said there were guys at his rugby clinic who would have the hots for her when she helped out but were too terrified to talk to her. Lachy was the first one who really made the effort and he came along at the right time, when Geva was getting nearer to thirty. She always told me she wanted to start a family in her early thirties and I think there was a strong element of not wanting to let go of this guy. A "Could he be the one? Full steam ahead!" mentality. Geva's personality changed when she was with him, without question. We had a conversation before the wedding and she questioned whether she was doing the right thing. She actually asked me, "Mum, should I be doing this?" and I said, "No. I don't think you should."*

'When Lachy brought Geva home to meet his mum for the first time she was everything Sue ever wanted in a daughter-in-law. She adored Geva – Sue was also a horse-rider and a netball nut and Lachy had brought home an ideal woman. It was like he thought "Geva will tick all the boxes for Mum, she will love her."

Whenever I went over to visit them or they would travel over to the UK – like for the Com Games in 2014 – we were always putting in so much effort to make him feel welcome and part of the family. But it didn't feel like he made as much effort with us. He just wanted to spend time with Geva.

Geva is so calm in an argument; she doesn't raise her voice easily. She would be trying to keep things calm, not adding to the argument by shouting and I honestly believe that probably infuriated him.

They did work on things and try to sort their relationship out, but to no avail. Lachy is very eloquent and a real charmer, and Geva somehow always ended up feeling like things were her fault. As her mum it was hard to watch.

'*In 2017, Geva was captain of Sunshine Coast Lightning and they played in the grand finals. That was a Sunday, and they won! And yet I had her on the phone to me in tears on the Monday morning as he had completely and utterly burst her bubble. Instead of being out there, enjoying the celebrations, she was sobbing on the end of the phone, a complete wreck. I don't even know what he said to her but that was it for me. When I was over there at the beginning of 2018 I told her enough was enough, she needed to get out of this relationship. And she knew it too.*'

So there you have it. In a nutshell, my wedding, my relationship and my divorce. It's probably best to get it all out in the open. Getting married to Lachy will always be my biggest regret and it embarrasses me that it happened. I am embarrassed because I never want to fail at anything in life but this I definitely did. I am embarrassed to tell people I was once married. I find it hard as I project such a strong, level-headed persona on court and yet I find myself, even now, getting emotional about that part of my life. When two people aren't right for each other, no amount of trying to make it work will solve anything. It does take two, I wasn't perfect, but I was fooling myself in always trying to see the good in our relationship and trying to change it, which just wasn't ever going to work.

I find it a struggle to talk about the fact that I was once married to him, but I suppose over time it will stop being this big failure in my mind and I can move on. I am happy to be out of that relationship and of course I want nothing but the best for Lachy, but the whole experience knocked my self-confidence. My self-esteem took a dive and it took a long time for my self-worth to start to recover. I didn't think anyone would want me, I didn't think any man would want my 'history'. It's funny, isn't it, how we completely doubt ourselves and our worth whether someone we love didn't love us back or because what started well just went wrong, or because we just weren't ever right for each other. For some reason we feel it's our fault, that we've failed. I thought I was an all-right person and yet now I believe the person I thought I was in love with didn't love me and that still hurts. I have become harder as time has moved on, less easily impressed, although I still am who I am and I know, when it comes to relationships, I give it my all and I do everything in my power for that person. I just hope, that someone will love me for me, will bring out the best in me, will look at me like there is no one else in the entire world. My heart might have been broken but I still believe in true love, I still want 'for ever' with someone.

* * *

But back to netball. After our disappointing Com Games, we were preparing for the Netball World Cup in 2015, which was being held in Sydney. It was a tough time for a lot of the girls and it took us a while to pick ourselves up again. It didn't help that England Netball decided to sack Anna Mayes as our coach. It just didn't go down well with the players, the way it was done. Whatever had happened between Anna and me in the past, I respected her as a coach and I think England Netball dumping her was a harsh and unfair call. Yes, we had a disappointing Games, but if anything it showed how close we were to causing a major upset. They appointed as head coach Tracey Neville, my former teammate, who had been assisting Anna for the past couple of years.

Tracey came in and in all honesty it felt like a bull in a china shop. She hadn't built up that rapport with the players, something that was part of Anna's coaching style – working with each individual, focusing on their strengths and weaknesses on court and their nerves and confidence off court. I think it took a while for the players to start to believe in what she was doing and settle themselves again. When she first came in, she was very headstrong and managed to piss off a lot of players and staff. She wanted to put her stamp on the team; she started running all these new programmes and changing routines and she was quite dominant. Being strong-minded isn't a bad thing in itself, though, as she sticks to her guns and you know where you stand with her! She has softened over the years and she has grown in confidence in the role too.

So, at the end of 2014 we had a new coach and a new challenge – to forget the mistakes of the Com Games and concentrate on kicking arse in the 2015 World Cup.

I'm not lying when I say that 2014 had its fair share of highs and lows, but one of the biggest highs for me was receiving my hundredth cap for England in December. A month before that momentous occasion I had been voted number-one netball player in the *Guardian*'s annual world top ten rankings. The panel of judges were big names in the world of netball, consisting of former national and international players, ex-England coaches and current coaches from other countries, TV pundits from the UK, Australia and New Zealand, university sports professors . . . it was an extensive and prestigious list and I was honoured to have been voted number one. I was also the only England player on the list. I couldn't believe I was now getting this recognition and this accolade, having missed out on playing for my country for nearly a year and a half.

My hundredth cap for England also came after completing my hundredth game in the ANZ Championship. I became the first import player to have reached such a milestone in the trans-Tasman competition, and ironically my hundredth game was against my former team, Thunderbirds, in Adelaide. It was such a cool situation; I don't think I ever thought when I first signed up for the league that I would be playing out there for so long! But Australia wasn't just where I was playing netball and improving my game. I was making great friends too, having great experiences and finding myself feeling more at home here than in England. I was really enjoying my time with Vixens. Having the right relationship with my goal defence, as I had with Sonia in England, was so important to me. I had it now with Bianca, the Vixens captain, too. It was definitely a combination we didn't have to work too hard at – it just clicked.

On 14 December 2014 I was to receive my hundredth England cap and I was hoping things would go a bit smoother than when I was due to receive my very first cap all those years ago. But this is England Netball we are talking about and nothing ever goes to plan! There was a bit of a debacle over the match as we were meant to be playing Malawi in a three-match series in Liverpool, but there was an issue with the team getting their visas, or something with their governing body, and they ended up not being able to make the flight over in time for the first game. But the series still went ahead and the Welsh national team stepped in and took their place for that match.

So there you have it. I got my hundredth cap against Wales and, without sounding big-headed, it meant we were pretty much guaranteed a win as the ranking difference between the two teams was quite substantial, so everything was a little bit more relaxed. But the best thing was that I was able to lead the team out on court. That honour normally falls to the captain but this time it was me and I was allowed to have my two half-sisters walk out either side of me too! Inez was only ten years old and Noor was eight and they were just my little mini-me's. They wore T-shirts that had 'Mentor' and '100' printed on the backs and it was the best feeling in the world to be able to walk out with them.

It was announced to the stadium why I was leading the team out and we got a massive round of applause and standing ovation as we came out. I loved having my sisters be part of that moment. I knew how cool it would be for them and I loved that not all eyes were on me – I hate being the centre of attention! Yes, of course it was great to have reached such an important milestone, but I'm not good when the spotlight is on me. I like to hide at the back normally! But I accepted that this was going to be one hell of an experience for Inez and Noor, and I was happy thinking it was a cool thing for them rather than a big thing for me.

Mum and Dad were both in the crowd and that in itself was quite special as it's not often I get all the family to a game. They watched as their children stood on court and sang the national anthem and got a standing ovation. I'm pretty sure they were bursting with pride! When Inez and Noor went back to Holland and into school, they told all their friends and teachers about it; they had TV clips to show and they were able to talk about me and netball, a sport that isn't very well known to the Dutch.

After the game I received a bunch of flowers but I think that was because I was named player of the match. I didn't get anything for my hundredth cap, other than that experience. Mum and I had organised everything that day because we didn't want to leave anything down to England Netball. Jade Clarke celebrated her hundredth cap at the Glasgow

Commonwealth Games and England Netball didn't do anything to mark it at all, so the rest of the girls and I made it special for her and made a fuss of her that game. In my case, I have only just managed to get my little medallion for my very first cap, for goodness sake, so I expect I will be a lot older when I finally get something for my hundredth cap – if anything at all! I did make sure all the girls signed my dress, though, and I have it framed. All the girls on the team had decorated the changing rooms as a surprise for me; there was a big '100' banner over my locker area and balloons and banners everywhere. It was a bit of a mess! Dad hadn't been to any of my games in Australia yet and only one or two in the UK, so it was great to have him there at such a momentous game. Inez and Noor are adamant that he needs to bring them over and watch the World Cup this year, which would be so cool. They haven't seen me play at a major event yet, so to have them there would be the icing on the cake.

The start of 2015 was just as magical as the end of 2014. I was back in Melbourne and driving to training with Vixens when I got a call from Tracey.

'Geva, I'm looking towards the World Cup . . . I want to offer you the captaincy role.'

And I would like to say my reply was dignified but I think I was more like, 'Oh . . . oh! SHIT! What?! Really?!'

'Will you take it?' she said.

'I'd be honoured!' I said. I think I was still in shock. 'I'm not used to being handed this sort of thing . . . is it something the players want?' I asked.

'To be honest, Geva, this is something I want,' said Tracey. 'I think you are the right person to lead the team.'

And that was that! It was a short phone call but what a life-changing moment. Me, England captain! Of course right away I wanted to ring Mum. I had no idea what time it was over there but I knew she wouldn't care.

When the announcement was made, it was like I was royalty or something. When I told people I was captain of the England netball team I was put on a bit of a pedestal. I think people still refer to me as captain of England now, and I feel a bit bad and I always correct them. 'No, not me any more!' I say. But it's quite funny, I suppose. And flattering!

Having been given the nod, it was all systems go and as I was based in Melbourne, a lot of the communicating with the England squad was done over the telephone or with Skype calls. I would be talking to everyone in the UK, everyone who played their part in the team – the staff, nutritionists, psychologists, the CEO, the personal trainers, members of the board. And I would sort everything out with Tracey, talking through and agreeing ideas and routines and everything with her. She likes her captain to have lots of involvement with the planning, the training and preparation. She likes to bounce ideas off the captain and you end up making quite a few decisions and having lots of control. I don't mind that as I am a control freak and I like to know a little about everything so I can see what's happening. This was important to me; as with whatever I do I want to give it all of my time, energy and commitment. But because I was on the other side of the world it did mean I had lots of 5 a.m. alarm wake-ups in order to speak to people and sort stuff out. I definitely had no idea being captain was so intense. It wasn't just leading the team out onto court on the day and chatting to players between quarters – it was like a full-time job! There is no accurate role description for it – you are always managing this or negotiating that or giving your opinion on something else. And you have a squad of twenty-four you are looking after, not just twelve. So that's a lot of people with a lot of individual concerns to deal with!

The World Cup came round and we headed off to Sydney. I remember we stayed in the Pullman Hotel for a week before our first game. Tracey's parents were flying over from England. They were due to arrive on the Wednesday and our first game was on the Friday. We got a phone call Wednesday evening saying that Tracey's dad had been taken into hospital; he had come off the flight very unwell and had had a heart attack and was on a life-support machine. Tracey's brothers got flown over to Sydney and although as captain I was aware of what was happening, the rest of the team didn't know anything was wrong. I spoke to them on Thursday, before our game the next day, and explained the situation. The leadership team, the assistant coach and I made sure we were organised and had planned everything, making sure the team was ready for the first game so Tracey could just concentrate on her family.

And on that Friday afternoon, we played. Tracey was there for the game in body but not in spirit. They had turned her dad's life-support machine off that morning. It was a very emotional game. It was a very emotional World Cup. Her mum and her brothers stayed on for a while afterwards because they wanted to support her. I knew she would be flying her dad's body back to the UK after the World Cup was over and I just felt so sad for her.

It was the most heartbreaking time we had ever had as a team. We knew what we had to do, we knew the task at hand and we were, to a certain extent, able to stick to that. We were making sure Tracey had distractions, that things were positive and upbeat in the team, but it was hard. It was incredibly draining for the whole group as everyone just felt such sadness for Tracey and her family. In that World Cup we played some of the toughest games we had ever played. Sonia, my best buddy, my GD partner in crime, was still in the team and as far as the pool games went, we did OK, but we played against New Zealand in the semi-finals and they beat us easily. I think it was probably by ten goals or so. We just weren't in the same contest. So that left us with Jamaica in the bronze medal play-offs. I had been here countless times before and, to be honest, I didn't see us mentally winning it. The game started to go the way I had predicted; we were just plodding along, everything was a battle. Jamaica had the momentum and the upper hand through most of the first two or three quarters. And then I remember they brought Sonia on as GD. And no word of a lie, she came on, she was very vocal and she made such a difference to the team performance. Her intercepts and turnovers and freshness just lifted the team completely and suddenly we were off and away! We ended up winning quite comfortably in the end, 66–44, and it was a great finish to what was the hardest and most emotional competition any of us had been involved in. We had won a medal for Tracey and for her dad.

Amid all this, Pam and I were honoured to be invited to a special event to tell us we had been inducted into the English Netball Hall of Fame. It was organised by the England Netball Supporters Club and it gave fans who had travelled down under a chance to meet us and the team. It was so surreal, I was being inducted into the Hall of Fame, but poor old mum who had travelled to Sydney to watch me play hadn't been given an invite! She and Eva heard about it, though, and gatecrashed! Their daughters had over two hundred England caps to their names and this was a momentous occasion – there was no way they were going to miss the evening celebration.

After the World Cup there was a bit of a break for us. Tracey chose different captains for different series matches, and the captaincy changed hands a few times and then I think they decided they wanted someone who was based in the UK. I understood that; there was a lot going on there and the schedules were tight. Tracey had developed the

Mum and Raoul are massively important to me; the relationship I have with them is like no other and it is stronger than any other relationship I will ever have.

I think the world of my dad and I have a huge amount of respect for him, here we are on holiday in Minorca.

'Can you join us, Geva? Just stand there and wave your arms and look scary . . .'
Where my netball career began at St Peter's School in Bournemouth.

I didn't think long about joining Team Bath and ended up playing
with them for ten years winning the Super League three times.

My first Commonwealth Games in Manchester in 2002 was unlike anything I had ever experienced before, the atmosphere was unreal.

My move to Adelaide in 2008 caused a bit of a stir, but it was the best thing I could have done for my netball.

The 2010 Commonwealth Games in Delhi was certainly an interesting experience.

Thunderbirds won the ANZ Championship in 2010 and it was a great way to round off my time in Adelaide.

My trip to Bali to chill out during a bye week soon turned into a much bigger drama – 'The Bali Four' were pulled apart by the media and it was the beginning of the end of my time in Adelaide.

noved to play with the
elbourne Vixens in 2010
d was elated to win the
emiership in 2014.

Kadeen Corbin blamed herself for our loss
against the Silver Ferns at the 2014 Commonwealth Games, but one mistake doesn't make
a loss and we win together, we lose together,
we hurt together. We ride the emotions – the
highs and the lows – as a team.

'e won a bronze medal at
he 2015 World Cup, which
as the hardest and most
notional competition any
us had been involved with.

My name had been put forward to be the flag bearer at the 2018 Commonwealth Games, in the end the flag was carried by the triathlete Alastair Brownlee, but he was mobbed by netball players the whole time!

There aren't many moments in my life that I can remember in such vivid detail b
I can honestly say, that Commonwealth Games on the Gold Coast when we were t
with Australia until the final few seconds of the game – I think I will have that
moment tucked away somewhere safe in my mind for ever.

The gold medal presentation was a bit of a blur but I remember as soon as the England flag went up we were all in floods of tears.

Me and my Lightning team mates dressed in our national kits: England, Australia, NZ and South Africa – netball forges true friendships all around the world.

Moving to Collingwood Magpies has been great for me professionally and personally, I met Mason who plays for the AFL team.

My wonderful mum is my biggest supporter, she's been there for me throughout my whole career and our relationship the most important thing in the world.

Netball is a sport that demonstrates dedication, teamwork, skill and perseverance. It's a game that shows nerves of steel and wills to win and it's a game I'm so proud to be part of.

England programme so that the people playing out in Australia and New Zealand would come back two weeks before an international, train in the training camp and then go into test series mode, or Commonwealth Games mode or World Cup mode, depending on what was happening. That is the point when Ama Agbeze took over the reins as captain and she did a great job. But it definitely took its toll on her, as it has on captains before. I think we netball players can do a lot better in the way we support our captains, as a team and as a bigger organisation. There is a lot of work involved and we rely on them a lot. Mum calls captaining a poisoned chalice and she advised me that if I was ever offered it again I should think long and hard before I took it!

Life with the Vixens in 2015 had gone from high to low. We had won the year before with Bianca Chatfield as our captain, but this year we got the premiership curse. The year 2016 didn't start off much better for us; I think we ended up at the end of the season bumming out in third or fourth position. Simone McKinnis, a very good former Diamonds wing defence, had been the coach when Julie Hoornweg left in 2014 but it felt like there was a lot of change in the air. The league was changing too.

The ANZ Championship saw netball become a semi-professional sport in Australia and New Zealand, which meant increased media coverage and player salaries. Netball Australia were looking to create a bigger, nationally exclusive league with significantly improved broadcasting and media deals. It still had the same teams from Australia involved, but three new teams joined the league too. New Zealand formed their own successor league, the ANZ Premiership, which is contested by six teams based in New Zealand.

At the beginning of the season that year, I had a conversation with Vixens that started something like this: 'Geva, you're getting on a bit . . .'

I was thirty-two years old. I had a few wear-and-tear problems with my knees and the previous year I'd had a scope on my left knee, which is basically just a clean-out because I had lots of floating fragments. Now my right knee needed a good clean-out too. Instead of the swelling staying in the front of my knee, it 'pulled' round to the back of my knee and I developed a Baker's cyst, a large swelling at the back of my knee.

I used to go into a clinic every four or five weeks to have surgery to get my knee aspirated. I had to lie on my tummy and they would find the bulging bit and put a needle in to suck out the fluid in the back of my knee. There was no anaesthetic involved. Sometimes there was a little bit of puffiness at the front too, so they would suck that out as well. Mum was with me once when I was having it done. She couldn't handle it at all. I think the doctors were worried about her – she was turning green! There was a big difference for her between me describing it and her actually seeing it happen – I think she felt bad that I was being put in so much pain on a regular basis. But the treatment has always worked brilliantly and I feel so good afterwards! I can move my knees with no aches or pains. I can't thank the Olympic Park Team enough for all the care they've given me.

I also had platelet-rich plasma (PRP) treatment, which acts as an anti-inflammatory. In a nutshell, doctors would take out some of my blood, spin it, and then put the white blood cells back. I had this for most of 2016 and, again, it wasn't pleasant but the results were worth it.

I suppose, in a sense, the Vixens were looking at the bigger picture. They were being honest with me and I did appreciate that. I was getting old in their eyes and I'd had a few injuries, a few niggles. They told me that they'd like to keep me around, maybe on a year-long contract, but that they saw me in more of a 'mentoring' role. They wanted me to focus my attention on girls who were up and coming and needed someone to nurture them.

Now don't get me wrong, I am not opposed to helping others in the team – I like that, I enjoy that and I think it is a good way to push both of us for a playing position. I had already spent time mentoring and nurturing some of the younger girls like Emily Mannix and Jo Weston (they are both now Diamonds players) and guiding them through the game. But I didn't want to do just that because I didn't feel like I was done playing yet. I was still very competitive – I am still competitive! It was two years to the next Commonwealth Games and I wanted to play in it. I needed to carry on getting court time and playing at a top level. What they were offering was a defence-coach position, which meant reduced court time and a reduction in salary.

But then along came rugby. I was approached by Melbourne Storm, the National Rugby League team in Melbourne, to help them with a video-advert campaign. Rugby union and rugby league struggle to get the attendance that netball, AFL and soccer get, so I was called upon, along with a guy called Nick Maxwell, the Collingwood FC premiership captain, and Molly Meldrum, a well-known Australian musician, to persuade people that whatever 'code' you came from, meaning what area of Melbourne, you could still support Melbourne Storm. It was great fun to be part of the ad and it had such a good, fun vibe to it. It wasn't long after the ad that the team got in contact with me again; Melbourne Storm NRL club had put in for a licence to start up their own netball team, and together with the University of the Sunshine Coast they formed the Sunshine Coast Lightning. The formation of the team came about as the league changed from ANZ to the new Suncorp Super Netball league and I was asked, did I want to be involved in this brand-new team? They had recruited Noeline Taurua, known as Noels, who was a New Zealand coach and assistant coach for the Silver Ferns. And it was like they had just spoken the magic words.

I had heard some great things about Noeline being an amazing coach who had a very holistic approach. So I was very intrigued. She called me and I remember we talked for over an hour – about everything apart from netball! The biggest thing that sold it for me was that the team she was putting together on the Sunshine Coast would be a collection of people with the best stats – most deflections, most pick-ups, high percentage of shots, and the ones with the best netball traits that together would make a great team. Combined with the fact that the people she had in mind were players she believed would all mix well personality-wise, it was sounding like a very healthy, strong and exciting team that I definitely wanted to be part of. To cut a long story short, I loved everything she was saying. I think in the end it was probably quite a tough decision to leave Vixens, because they had been good to me and I had a good relationship with Simone. But then again, I didn't want to stay with them and not play elite netball. I still had a fire in my belly to win and now I was ready for something new and completely different.

I moved to the Sunshine Coast in November 2016 and it meant leaving Lachlan behind in Melbourne. That was good. This move probably couldn't have come at a much better time for me; I needed to get away. I think we both needed some time apart. Besides, his school was in Melbourne and he was teaching full-time, so he couldn't have moved away that easily. I don't think Vixens knew how bad the marriage was, to be honest, and I wonder if they might have made more of an effort with me if they had. I think initially they didn't think I would leave the club as it meant leaving my husband behind, so potentially they might have put forward a better offer. But it didn't matter. I had my heart set on a new start, a new team and a new challenge.

11 GEVA AND THE SEVEN DWARFS

'There are far, far better things ahead than any we leave behind.'
C. S. Lewis

WHEN I first moved to Lightning, Noeline told us she had selected a skeleton of a team. She went for experience across the court with a strong person at the attacking end, a strong mid-quarter and a strong defender. The mid-quarter was from New Zealand, Laura Langman. She still holds the title for the most capped player for the Silver Ferns, a record previously held by Irene van Dyk. Making up the attacking end, Noeline had recruited Caitlin Bassett, who is the current Australian Diamonds captain. I had faced Caitlin on many occasions – we have battled it out against each other in the goal circle countless times before – so it was quite cool to think she was on my team now! She was ready for a change too, and after years of playing against each other we'd be putting on the same dresses and fighting for the same result. Well, as Lightning teammates that is; I knew the rivalry would come back next time I met her in my Roses dress!

I'm a naturally organised person, so when I arrived I took on the role of setting a few things up and helping everyone out. Laura, Caitlin and I formed a bit of a leadership group and both Laura and I thought the natural choice would be to select Bass as captain. She and I were both very supportive of this; we told Noels the same thing: she was a big star in Australia and a phenomenal player and we would be happy for her to lead us in this competition. Even the media were making hints, running stories about her being made captain, and whenever other teams were interviewed about this new Lightning team, they assumed that Bass would be in charge, even though nothing had formally been announced. But then our players got wind of what was going on and they wanted to have their say on who should be their captain. So Noeline set up a vote.

It was a new club so there needed to be a lot of new procedures put in place, including this one. They decided to split the vote so that the players' vote would account for 50 per cent of the vote and the other 50 per cent would come from the staff – the CEO, the coach and assistant coach. The top three names ended up being Bass, myself and Laura. Noeline then wanted to interview us for the position, so we each had to prepare a presentation about why we would make a good captain. It was the most terrifying thing I'd ever had to do! I think I had one or two sleepless nights in the lead-up to it and I don't know why; it wasn't like I had a strong desire to be captain, but I suppose, like with anything I do, I wanted to do a good job. But the more I prepped, the more nervous I got and I realised I did want this captaincy role, the role I wasn't initially fussed about! Everything was fine when I was in the interview. I think all the stressing out beforehand was because I was worried that I wouldn't present myself well. But in the end it went well. I told the panel all the things I would personally bring to the role and I think I conveyed the most important message – that it would be a massive honour to lead the team. The next day I got a call from Noeline congratulating me on being captain! It was an incredible feeling. I had been voted for by my teammates, the coaches, the staff and the CEO and that made it even more special. It gave me the confidence to lead and be myself, knowing that the team had that faith and trust in me. It highlights the one thing we don't do as well as an England side – in our set-up it is just the coach who chooses the captain. And that isn't to say our captain isn't great, but as a captain, it's an incredible feeling to know you have also had the nod of approval from your teammates.

I got flown to Sydney the next day, as the league had put on a launch day and were bringing in all the captains from the eight different teams. We took part in TV interviews and had photos, there were lots of speeches and it was all quite a fun way to mark the start of the season.

The funniest thing for me was that all the other captains

there that year were middies (mid-court players) and all of a certain height. Then I rock up as the new Lightning captain, all six foot two inches of me, and I think the waiting photographers quickly realised how funny this would look and started calling us Geva and the Seven Dwarfs! There are some great photos out there of that.

Mainly I remember being just so excited and honoured and ready to get my teeth into this new challenge. All the other captains were very supportive of me and congratulated me, which was brilliant. Although I do remember one of them asking me why my dress looked so different from the others as it was just a very plain dress with the logo of the club, a lightning strike, on the front and back. The difference was that we didn't have any sponsors yet as we were a brand-new team and no one wanted to take a chance on us. Sponsors don't like taking a risk and would prefer to stick with the more established teams. We didn't even have any offices or anything to begin with; we had a temporary room at the university, one or two staff members, coaches and players and that was pretty much it. We had to build up everything from scratch. All credit to Lightning, they did manage to recruit some of the best people in their fields, from Kurt and Greg, our physios, to Mark, our strength and conditioning coach, to Anthony, the whizz behind the camera, and Kellie, our nutritionist. We were fortunate enough to be able to use the facilities at the university and also some of their staff to cover some roles. But otherwise, no one really paid us much attention. I don't think anyone would have predicted that this new team, built from scratch, with limited resources, no sponsors and a novice English captain, would ever win the premiership. We felt underestimated, a new team in a league of established teams with lots of money behind them.

Our first game saw us up against our state rivals, the Queensland Firebirds, who had been very successful in previous years. We ended up getting a draw for our first game and that was a good outcome.

People often ask me if heckling or sledging happens in netball. There is no space for booing in netball in my mind; it shouldn't happen. I understand that crowds get emotional and overexcited and carried away but it's unacceptable when you are targeting an individual player. But does it happen? Of course it does. The first season we played as Lightning we went across to Perth to play against Fever. Bass had previously played for the club; she was their top goal-scorer and had played as a junior before moving her way up through the club to the top level. And then she moved clubs and came to us. When she went out against Fever in that first game, she was booed the moment her foot stepped on to that court. I was shocked. It was horrible for her. I can't remember exactly what was shouted but there was just lots of jeering and booing and taunting. I wasn't going to stand for it and when I was interviewed at the end – as both captains are – I absolutely laid into the crowd. I told them how disappointed I was in them and how disrespectful they were in their behaviour towards this girl who had given them so much netball over the years.

Netball is not a place where we want or tolerate heckling, booing, sledging – leave it to us players on court. I got on my soapbox as I felt very passionate about it and I made sure everyone knew how cross I was. I was also very protective of Bass, who took it all very well, considering. She is a tough cookie and very thick-skinned. But I was reeling. The behaviour of the crowd hurt me and I was upset for her. Normally after a game I make sure I spend a lot of time with the spectators, and I will go around and sign autographs and take photos, but I made a point of not doing it that time as I was furious about the way they'd treated one of my own. Bass actually got player of the match that game, which was awesome – and a big two-fingers-up at the crowd!

I'm not saying that we are so precious we can't cope with a bit of heckling, but it's just not needed in our sport. Of course we do get hecklers. They tend to flock around the goalposts and attack the shooters, saying nasty things when they miss a shot. But the majority of the crowd are pretty good at telling these few to shut up or calling for security so they can be removed. Shooters are more sensitive souls and they have enough things to block out already when they're making a shot, never mind someone calling 'Miss!' as the ball is about to leave their fingers.

Now, when it comes to heckling on court, there are some particular players in this league who will drop comments during play. They'll stand round the circle edge and they'll be like, 'Oh, umpire, can't you see that?' or 'Did you see her pushing?!' or 'Good pass!' when the ball goes off the back line. I don't say anything myself; defenders don't really say anything unless we are shouting out encouragement. The ones who do it tend to be the middies and, to be honest with you, I don't know how they have the energy to throw cheeky comments about – they obviously aren't working hard enough!

We had got off to a good start in the league and after a few wins we started to get noticed a bit more, which meant most weeks we had to hand our dresses back to add to the growing number of sponsor logos we were accumulating. They bought into our club and wanted to be part of our team, and by the end of the season we were full! The thing that I enjoyed most about our team was that we really did create it from scratch – we had devised our own values and culture and built a foundation for the years to come. It was the first national team the Sunny Coast had and that meant everyone got behind us too; we had a great community feel.

I remember the first time we played my old side, the Melbourne Vixens, they travelled to our home court and although we didn't start well and were down at half-time, we ended up winning. In my book that is always good because you always want to be able to beat the team you've just moved from! It's a satisfying feeling. You want to feel like you have proved something to yourself, you are moving forward in your game, you are bettering yourself. We lost a few games, we won a few more – the ones we won were important ones, sentimental ones, and as the season progressed we were looking pretty good and sitting in a strong position on the ladder.

The Giants, based in Sydney, were another new team and they ended up being our rivals. Unfortunately for them they lost their captain Kim Green to injury, which left a huge hole in the team. She was an amazing sportswoman and a few years later, when England won gold at the Commonwealth Games, she made sure she went and found Mum in the crowd and gave her a big hug. She told Mum that I deserved every moment of that victory, which, as an Australian and having just witnessed her country lose, was an incredibly generous thing for her to say.

On the couple of occasions we had previously met the Giants, the matches had been a real battle. We'd be going goal-for-goal in each game, which made it so tense yet thrilling.

We had a good season, improving with every game, which was our motto – to be better than the week before. We finished the regular season in a strong position in the table, sitting second, which meant we got into the finals. It was the start of a crazy couple of weeks for us and we travelled to Melbourne to play Vixens on their home court. They finished top of the table ahead of us. We came from behind to win the match by one goal, which meant we faced a home grand final against Giants. You just want to hit another level come finals and that is what it felt like we did. It's hard to pinpoint exactly why it all went right (if I could I would bottle it!) but everything just worked, everything clicked. We hit our stride and no one could touch us. We talked about that in our mindfulness and psychology sessions – what that feeling is like when everyone is on the same page. And to have a team of individuals, all in sync – it was a feeling you can't really describe. Everything slows down around you and you are just grinding away all together. We ended up winning by seventeen goals, which was incredible. To finish the season off like that, well, like it was a fairy tale!

We were a new team, we had taken a risk, we had come together as a lot of individuals from different states, different backgrounds, different countries, and we had managed to make it work against all odds and in a competition that, at the start, probably hadn't really accepted us properly. We won the premiership in our inaugural season. I hope one day someone makes a film about this team and this journey. It would be a blockbuster!

Karla Pretorius, a phenomenal South African player, was my goal defence and we just 'got' each other right away. I thrive off my connection with Karla, and I love how much she has developed her game and grown in confidence. I am proud to watch her when she plays with South Africa. Yes, it's to England's detriment, but at the end of the day she is a great player and a great person off court, and I want her to do well.

I took the role of captain very seriously but I didn't try to be someone I'm not. I like to have fun and I also like to make sure all the girls on the team feel valued and to lead by example. I was keen to have an environment where everyone felt they could have a voice, but also had enough trust in me to know I would make the right decisions. I wasn't perfect but I like to think I did an OK job.

Throwing myself into the new team and captaincy was what I needed. Being apart from Lachy due to my netball commitments was a blessing. Things felt better between us when we were apart.

It's funny to think that although in my industry I have to be strong and confident and a positive leader, I can feel the opposite in my personal life. I often felt sad, empty and deflated by our relationship and the negative environment it created. In a sporting context, I would stand up for what I believed in, I would be strong, I would be confident; and yet in my own home with my own husband those behaviours were absent.

You don't realise at the time how weak you have become, you just accept it. It was what it was. Now I think to myself, what was I thinking? It is hard for an athlete to admit failure and what you learn in a professional capacity – to play to win – you bring to your personal life too. I didn't want to 'fail' at my marriage and so I did a lot of things because I thought it would somehow make everything better. I went along with the wedding because I had planned it and it was at a time in my life when I thought this was what I should be doing. I have learned now that it is OK to say no, it is OK to rock the boat and not worry if that upsets other people, and it's OK to admit defeat sometimes, although that is hard for an athlete to accept! I have to remind myself that I am a strong, independent woman first and foremost and that I need to trust my gut more and stop trying to please others. Life is too short; you have to give everything your all, yes, but you also have to accept when it just isn't working. I think we both knew that our marriage wasn't working and it was over, but neither of us wanted to acknowledge it.

Things got worse when my brother, who was playing basketball locally in Melbourne, hurt his foot. His visa was coming to an end and he had just arranged for a new one to go and work in New Zealand for the next two years. He flew over to New Zealand and looked to base himself there, but his foot didn't get any better. He turned out to be suffering from a Lisfranc fracture. I said to him, 'Right, we need to get this sorted,' and I flew him to the Sunshine Coast to be treated by the Lightning medical team, which is something I would do for any member of my family or any close friend who needed it. The team were amazing and helped devise an action plan for his recovery. A few scans showed that he had to have quite a major operation on his foot, with a twelve-month recovery period. He is a tall, solid lad and needed time to heal so he could move around before he even thought about playing sport again, so he stayed with me. Lachlan didn't seem to understand that I would always help and support my family, just like I would his, and all I wanted him to do was to get that and be part of it.

Having my brother around was a huge comfort as Lachy and I were arguing a lot – I was in tears most nights while I was talking to him. I said to him that I was happy to pay for some of Raoul's surgery and medical costs up front and my family would pay us back. 'I have an Australian bank account,' I said, 'I earn money too.' And that was the hardest thing. I earned that money and I am entitled to spend it how I want to. I don't go out shopping, I don't fritter it away. I spend money on what I need. Money caused us endless issues and arguments on the phone each evening and it was so draining. And meanwhile I was trying to manage and lead a team, make sure I was still training and performing and doing my studies too. The grand final when we won the season was on a Sunday and I was on a complete high. Until I spoke to him. I rang my mum on Monday in tears.

If my personal life was torturing me, in a sense you could say my netball life was saving me. I came away at the end of the Suncorp Super Netball season and straight into a Quad Series with England. We finished third, which we were pleased with, behind the big hitters Australia and New Zealand but above South Africa. We also competed in a Fast5 competition, which is a bit like Twenty20 in cricket; it's a five-player match and each quarter only lasts six minutes. The competition is held over three days and the first two days you play in a round-robin format. Then the four highest-scoring teams play in a finals day. It's fun, it's fast, and we seemed to adapt to its rampant pace easily. We ended up beating Jamaica in the final and it topped off not only a successful tournament for us but an extremely fun one. There was lots of dancing and singing and I played with my hair in bunches! It just finished off the winning streak for me that year. Well, not quite, as it turned out. I received an invitation to attend the Netball Australia awards; I had been nominated in two categories, Player of the Year and Best Goal Keeper. My professional fairytale year was about to get even more magical.

It is very bizarre as an English international to be invited to the Netball Australia awards. Although I am dual nationality, having received my citizenship on Australia Day in 2016, I still felt a little bit of an intruder. That year they were also celebrating the twenty-five-year history of Netball Australia; all their previous playing dresses were displayed in frames and it felt extra special. The awards were held at the town hall in Melbourne and just to be there and be acknowledged was pretty awesome. It was quite humbling to be among people in and from Australia with them celebrating me, an international.

Sitting round the table representing Sunshine Coast Lightning were myself, Lachy, Bass, who had been named Diamonds captain again, our coach Noeline and her husband, our CEO Danielle Smith and her partner.

When the Coach of the Year award nominations were read out, I think everyone in that room – and certainly everyone on our table – expected Noels to be the winner. Absolutely, 100 per cent, no contest, hands down, she should have won it. But she didn't. I don't know what Netball Australia were thinking. Maybe they didn't want to acknowledge her performance because she was from New Zealand? Whatever the reason, it left a nasty taste in our mouths. Everyone could see that it should have been her. And yet they gave it to the Vixens' coach, Simone, who had previously played for Australia and was a product of the Australia coaching pathway. Not to take anything away from her, but it did not seem fair or right.

When the Suncorp Super Netball Best Player of the Year award came up I think I was still a little aggrieved for Noeline and I'm pretty sure I didn't think I would ever win. I knew I'd had a good year and people had mentioned that I was a strong contender, but I still didn't think it would be me. And then the presenter, Pete Lazer, announced my name! I hadn't planned a speech, so I just winged it and I was lucky enough that Pete knew netball and me well enough that when he handed the mic over I felt comfortable enough to just speak from the heart and say whatever came into my mind. I was still in complete shock, but I thanked a lot of people and I acknowledged a lot of people – although I probably forgot to thank and acknowledge a whole lot more! I think I got a laugh too when I held up the award and said, 'This is for the over-thirties!' We had been a little deflated after Noeline missed out on her award, so this definitely picked up the mood and gave us something to celebrate. And when I won Best Goalkeeper of the Year too it just topped off a pretty unbelievable night.

When I first moved up to Sunshine Coast I was living with a lady who I knew through a friend of a friend of Mum's – good old Mum is great when it comes to chatting to the right people. I then moved into another place a bit closer to the beach that I found on a site called flatmates. com. Wayne Buxley owned a four-bedroom house and needed a lodger. He was also English and he had moved to Adelaide, then to Melbourne, and then made his way up to the Sunshine Coast, just like me. It was like I was destined to be his lodger! He was a trainee pilot so he was away a lot, so it was a perfect living arrangement. I lived with him from 2017 to 2018. Lachy and Wayne didn't have much in common – but Wayne and my brother got on brilliantly well. Wayne witnessed several tearful phone calls between myself and Lachy but he was always good at offering support without interfering. I remember after another tearful argument with Lachy. Wayne tried to boost my confidence a little. 'Lach's got a racehorse, not a pony, with you, Geev, he should bloody look after you like one.' It made me laugh!

Sharing a house was good for a while but after about a year I decided it was time to get a little place for myself and start to settle. I was really loving the Sunshine Coast; I loved the community feel of the place and I had made some wonderful friends. Everyone was so welcoming and I felt so embraced by the locals. In a strange twist of fate I made friends with an ex-England player, Chrissie Browne, who had been axed from the netball team in 1999. She and her clan made me feel like part of their family. She helped me set up Netty Girls, an initiative that involved visiting primary schools in the neighbourhood and running netball workshops. I was so happy when I found my own little place near Birtinya, overlooking the waterways. It was so nice to feel like I had set up a home. Having somewhere that was home has been the most important thing for me throughout my years of playing and travelling back and forth between the UK and Australia.

At the beginning of 2018, Lachy decided to go on a sabbatical from work and come up to stay with me. We hadn't had a good Christmas and then I had the Quad Series in the UK in January, during which I was away for about a month, and we didn't speak for the entire time. It was a bit of a relief to have that break, to be honest. When I got back we had a discussion. We agreed that it wasn't working and basically decided to call it a day, and kind of lived like housemates for a couple of months. I was conscious of him having all this time off work and I didn't want him to waste it, so I suggested he book himself a trip away. He had always wanted to go to Japan so I tried to encourage him to do that. But he is one of those people who isn't always comfortable doing things by himself and prefers to have someone with him. He did go to Japan for three weeks and, again, we didn't really speak in that time. When he got back he packed up his stuff, went to stay with his brother for a bit, and then went back to Melbourne. Our marriage was over and the divorce proceedings would be starting soon.

12 GOING FOR GOLD

'If you don't see yourself as a winner, then you cannot perform as a winner.'
Zig Ziglar

THE Commonwealth Games 2018. My fifth Games. It felt like it was going to be a home Games for me, as it was being held on the Gold Coast, which was only a couple of hours' drive south from me, also on Australia's east coast. It also meant that when Mum flew in from the UK and my brother came over from New Zealand, they were able to stay with me and then get to the Games relatively easily. Mum got herself a little Airbnb place and was all set up to come and watch every match. I think she knew I might need a little extra support this year and it was good to have her and Raoul nearby.

Our England manager, Paul Dring, flew over a couple of months before the Games to check out the athletes' village and do a bit of a recce. He called me and asked me if I wanted to join him and some of the other Team England management group and my response was, 'Of course I bloody well do!'

I jumped in the car right after training, drove down through Brisbane, and met him on the Gold Coast. It was really cool to be able to walk around the village without any of the other athletes there, like a 'behind-the-scenes' look. The purpose of me being there was to help Paul write his report from a player's perspective, so he could report back to the team. A month or so later, when I was back in England at the training camp, he gave his presentation to the team and talked about the accommodation and the set-up and the different areas and I was able to contribute. I also had my uses – in some of the rooms you could ask for bed extensions for taller athletes, so all the managers had asked me to lie down on the beds to give them a visual guide to bed length. It was quite amusing, me having a little lie-down as we toured round all the beds!

To say England Netball's campaign got off to a strange start is probably an understatement. First of all, we had a training camp in Sydney to attend. We were all meant to meet there for a week before the Games but things were a little controversial for me as Lightning, who I was in pre-season training with at the time, had a three-day camp in New Zealand for all their players. England were to fly over the team members who were not aligned with a Suncorp Super Netball team and weren't already in Australia, and we SSN players were told to join the team a day after they landed. Lightning and I tried to negotiate whether I could do a day and a half in New Zealand with the team, as I was captain and would normally have a lot of input into our pre-season camp, and then come and join the England girls a day late. The coaches, Tracey and Noeline, ended up at a stalemate. Neither were prepared to budge, and in the end it was decided that I would just go straight to Sydney to the England camp and forget New Zealand. I'm not sure how it was resolved but Tracey is headstrong and you don't want to cross Noeline, so I'm sure it was interesting!

Rather frustratingly, the week in Sydney ended up being the biggest waste of time. We didn't get going until day three or four as we had to wait for some of the girls to get over jet lag. Then there wasn't much time for training; I think we had just a couple of gym sessions before heading straight into some practice matches. These were against two other teams in the Suncorp Super Netball League, the GWS from Sydney and the Sydney Swifts, both of whom are extremely good and who I'd obviously come up against in the season. A couple of the English girls who played for those teams in the league were allowed to play for them rather than be in the England team, which didn't seem right to me; surely the whole team should have been training and playing together from the start? And we got our arses well and truly kicked. We lost by about thirty goals one day and thirty-five goals the next.

Talk about deflated. England, the national team, about to compete at the Commonwealth Games, and we had lost

211

to two Australian club sides. It was demoralising to say the least. It completely broke us. I called Tracey out after the second game and a thirty-five goal loss while everyone was sat in a circle cooling down. I had had enough and I asked her, in front of everyone, 'What is going on?!' I was just furious. 'This isn't helping us,' I said, 'what is the point of getting some of our girls to play against us? What do we get out of this? This is about us as a team, us as a team trying to prepare for the Coms!'

The girls were silent, Tracey was silent. I continued. 'Tracey, we need to train together. We need to go through a bit of a game-plan, have some structure, then we can go out and play. Not just come away from all our different club sides and just automatically think we can gel as the England team!'

My rant was over. I think she was a bit taken back by it all. She tried to respond but then realised she had no leg to stand on and said she would speak to Ama, our captain. This was unlike me – I am normally a lot more tactful – but this was my fifth Games and it meant so much to me. When I spoke up to our coach in front of the whole team I was hoping that I was speaking on behalf of everyone; I thought I had a pretty good idea that we all felt the same. I had talked to some of the girls after our first practice match and some of them were in tears. They were doubting their ability, their self-confidence was knocked. While I was addressing Tracey I also spoke directly to the group. I remember asking, 'Guys, if you don't agree with me, speak up, please.' But they were all nodding and saying, 'No we do, we agree.'

Ama, our captain, came up to me afterwards and was very grateful. We ended up having a bit of a joke about it all and someone said, 'Wouldn't it be funny if after all this, losing in our practice games to a club team by thirty-five goals, we end up winning the gold medal!' Oh how we laughed! What a joke. And that was the end of that.

We had one more practice game lined up for the next day and this time we made sure we had an hour's training session all together before we played. It made such a difference – we came out and we played really well. We had a bit more of a boost when Chelsea Pitman's parents treated us all to a boat ride round Sydney Harbour. It was a bit of light relief after a fairly emotional and stressful few days and we loved it! We got our England kit while we were in the Sydney camp too. The dresses were a bloody nightmare as they didn't fit at all and it looked like we were wearing sacks! If you look good, you feel good, you play good. No one wants to go out on court looking like they are wearing ill-fitting gear – what does that say about the team? That we can't even sort out our kit?! The rest of the kit was fine but our match dresses were unwearable.

We got a seamstress on to it, and she pinned and stitched and added more material to the length and made all the alterations that had to be made. I basically needed two dresses sewn together as mine was like a swimsuit made for a toddler – far too short and tight! Because she took them away to work on, we didn't end up getting them back until the morning of our first match. I'd like to say this was a one-off, but there seems to be a problem with our dresses every time. I don't think I've ever had one World Cup or Com Games where we haven't had issues with them. It is beyond ridiculous. At the Commonwealth Games in Manchester the dresses were so awful that Mum called in her trampolining friend who used to design and make my leotards to alter them all. I genuinely think the designers seem to forget we are tall, athletic women or something. We always need to have extra length added and we are female so we always need to have a bit of shape for our hips. Some of our trousers have sometimes been like ankle-swingers or come up to mid-shin. You would have thought that they had got the gist by now – we are netballers, we are tall!

So that was our week's camp in Sydney and it was horrible and demoralising but we were England, we get on with it.

It was time to move to Brisbane for another holding camp with Team England. It was there that we had arranged to play Lightning. But that match got cancelled, I think because of what had happened beforehand with me in the New Zealand camp. To this day it seems to me there is still a little bit of angst between Noels and Tracey, although they're totally professional about it as they see each other quite often as coaches of their national sides!

So we were in Brisbane, in the holding camp. The basketball team were there, and the athletics guys and girls were there, and it was brilliant. Team England had such a vibe! The camp was right in the middle of Brisbane and as we walked around there was such a sense of excitement in the air. We carried on training hard and it was much more positive; it was just what we needed. We needed that time as a team. We were there for five or six days and then it was time to head an hour south to Gold Coast and be checked into the village. You get to select who you want to share rooms with and I was sharing with Eboni, the goal defence, who I get on really well with and who has similar routines to me. This is important as you need to be with someone you'll be comfortable with in tight quarters for an intense and pressured period of time. There were two apartments, with three bedrooms in each apartment and two beds in each room. The village had a good vibe to it as always. I had been before so I didn't have to spend a few days finding my way around – I knew where things all were. I hit the swimming pool as soon as we arrived. The complex was as cool as I remembered. Being here in the holding camp beforehand was good as we had chance to make friends and form bonds with other athletes; when you get to the village everything is so super-huge, you'd struggle to get to know people properly. I met up with lots of people from Team England who I recognised and had made friends with previously, along with other nations. And I know lots of people who play for New Zealand and South Africa and Australia too, obviously, so

I think this year I was bumping into lots of old faces – friends and foes! The best bit about the build-up to the Com Games is the last few days leading up to the opening ceremony. Everyone is relaxed and full of expectation and there is almost no pressure. I suppose there is a bit of sussing each other out, checking out the competition, but on the whole it is more about just enjoying ourselves. Then after the opening ceremony – bang! That's when all our competitive natures kick in.

There is always a voting poll for who they want Team England to have as a flag-bearer. Because this was my fifth Com Games, I was a bit of a front-runner for the honour. There were a few other athletes in contention, though, one of them being Alistair Brownlee. 'Well,' I thought, 'of course, if I'm going up against Alistair I'm never going to get the job!' But our manager Paul took it very seriously and he ended up printing off these little flyers with pictures of me, at all the different Com Games I'd been to, with the message 'Vote Geva!' He put them all round the hotel and tried to persuade all the managers in Team England to vote for me. He tried to get the basketball vote, the boxing vote . . . he was a man on a mission! The way it works is that in each sport the team discuss it and decide who they want – third preference, second preference and first – and the managers have the casting vote.

Anyway, despite the hearty campaign from my manager, Alistair ended up winning it. And rightly so – he is a great athlete and obviously a big name. The funny thing was, when it came to the opening ceremony, I'm quite embarrassed to say we literally mobbed Alistair as he came out! When you walk out on to the track for the first time at the ceremony you are all meant to be in lanes, but then as you walk out a bit further there is a bit of a scrum and a scuffle to get to the front and get to the cameras so everyone can be seen by their loved ones around the world. Every one of my England Netball teammates had the front patch on lockdown and we swarmed round Alistair like bees round a honeypot. There is the poor bloke, trying to carry the flag and wave, and he's basically being mobbed by twelve netballers! I was literally right next to him – I probably touched the flagpole I was that close – and I remember my mum saying afterwards, 'Jeez, Geva, you couldn't hold the flag but you couldn't have got much closer if you tried!' On camera and in all the photos the netball girls were front and centre and poor Alistair looked very bemused surrounded by this bevy of beauties!

Our first game was the day after the opening ceremony. We got presented with our dresses the morning of the match and they were perfect, thank goodness, and everyone was feeling positive and ready to perform. We started our campaign well; our first game was against Scotland and we won comfortably, 74–28. We then played Malawi, which was a little bit tougher, but we still won by thirty goals.

We felt at that point that everything was going well – the training that we had in between was really upbeat, our preparation was on track, we did our homework, we did our analysis . . . everything was working. And working well.

Then we had a bit of a test against Uganda. This is important to mention as we were doing well, we were on track for a comfortable win, and then they took me and Jo off to give us a rest and rotate some of the combinations. And then Uganda started coming back at us and we were totally unprepared! They have quite a good shooter and so they put me back on to put pressure on her and we did end up winning but only just, by about six goals. It was really close and this was still the group stages and we really didn't want to lose any matches. We had a tough draw; we had to work through the smaller-threat countries before we faced the biggest one in our pool, New Zealand. Although we had beaten them earlier in the year in the Quad Series at the Copper Box in London, we had never beaten them in a major tournament before, either a World Cup or Com Games. And yet beat them we did, by just under ten goals. It was so significant that people started to take note of us: 'OK, here are England now, top of their group, they have talked the talk, now they are walking the walk, they have come to play!' was pretty much the mood. And we had. We weren't here to mess around or make up numbers or come in third or fourth – we wanted to do well.

We are such a tight unit during a competition. We know what we are about and we don't let the media or anyone distract us. Everyone was on the same page. No one was overexcited that we had beaten New Zealand. It was good but we didn't really celebrate that win, we were more like, 'OK, yep, that's a tick in the box – next!'

I know that previously we had turned up and were a bit like, 'OMG, we are playing the Silver Ferns!', whereas now we were thinking, this is just another team, this is just another pool game, this is just the next step. There was no mental block to playing the Silver Ferns any more. Myself and a fair few other girls including Serena, Ama and Jo Harten, who had joined the Suncorp Super Netball league, were playing against girls we had trained with and played with week in week out and I think that helped. In fact, I know it helped; I knew there was no massive gap in ability any more. We didn't put them on a pedestal like we used to. I ran with them, I jumped with them, I threw with them. They are players and we are players. Tough games are not won in the first quarter; it is about grinding it down, it is about sticking it out. It's about knowing that momentum swings do happen, and whereas before that momentum would go against Team England and we would freeze, now we knew it was about the long game. We could get it back, we just had to keep going.

It was at this point in the competition that Tania, our assistant coach from Australia, had a brainwave. She had been with Thunderbirds when I played there and on occasion, to make me practise against the tallest of opponents, she had brought in Raoul as my training partner. When she heard that Raoul was here on the Gold Coast she called him in and set up some training practice for me to go against my six-foot-eleven brother. He took no prisoners and Eboni and I trained our socks off against him, knowing that we could use this opportunity to see how we could work against someone of his height. I can't tell you how cool it was having him there and being part of it all. He was our secret weapon!

Next up was Jamaica. It was the semi-final in a new venue and I felt like the crowd were probably more behind Jamaica than us. And it was a bloody tough game – we were down by seven goals at one point. I was up against Jhaniele, who is just a woman-mountain. She's an incredible athlete, not only tall at six feet six inches, but she can jump, she can shoot, she is very sturdy and she is hard to move. And trying to get the ball off her is very difficult, particularly when it's placed right in her hands. So that was the game. It was a tough first quarter and then, maybe in the second quarter, they managed to steam ahead. At half-time we were down but we just kept ploughing on and managed to keep ourselves in contention. And then we got down to the fourth quarter and I don't really know what happened but we managed to turn over enough balls to keep us going and everyone was doing their jobs – the shooters were managing to score, the mid-courters were bringing it down, and we were defending. We ended up, with seconds to go, with Jo having the ball in hand. She took a long shot, scored, and we won by one goal.

And it was at precisely that point when we all thought, 'This is it.'

Before, we had all been in teams where we had been a little complacent at this stage. We'd have been happy thinking, 'Hell, yeah! We are coming home with a medal!' We had never focused on getting gold, it was more, 'Well, at least we have something.' But now we meant business. Ama, Jo, Jade, Serena, Kadeen, Helen Housby and Eboni; we had all been at Glasgow four years ago, we were ready.

The end of that game signalled the battle cry, if you like. We were in it to win now. Nothing else would do. There is footage of me doing the most girly jump on the transverse line after that game. I was jumping around and skipping up and down because I was so excited – I knew we just had to get ourselves to this position to be unstoppable. This was our time.

Don't get me wrong, there were several times during the Jamaica game when we were losing and I was like, 'Shit, here we go again . . . back to the same old, same old.' But that thought didn't stay in my mind for long. I knew if we just kept going, kept chipping away collectively as a team, if we just kept working and working and chipping and chipping we could do it. There were no drastic coaching decisions made by us but there were some changes down the other end that worked in our favour. Tracey out-coached the Jamaican coach Arleene Findlay and it set us up for the final.

I remember Eboni and me going back to our bedroom after that match knowing we needed to get some sleep. But we were so hyped up – it is very hard to come down and start to chill out after a game, particularly a game that has just set you up into the final! As we were lying there – it was probably gone eleven now – we kept saying to each other, 'I can't sleep, can you? No!' We knew we needed to sleep, we knew we needed to get a good rest – especially as it was an early game the next day. Sorry, it was an early gold-medal final the next day!

Eventually we did get to sleep and the next day it was down to business. We arrived at the venue and the Jamaica and New Zealand games had already started. Jamaica were all over it and I remember feeling sorry for New Zealand. They were going to come away from the Com Games with nothing; it was going to be their worst ever performance. But I couldn't dwell on that. In our changing rooms we had a good vibe. Of course, there were lots of nerves too. I can only speak for myself but as soon as I take to the court, those nerves go and you forget about all the people watching and what it all means, and at the end of the day it's just about trying to do your job.

Initially, in the changing rooms, everyone is left to their own devices. People prepare for a game in different ways so it's important to let them get themselves ready. We focus, we calm ourselves, we strap up our ankles, we listen to one more song on our headphones, we repeat one more mantra in our head. Then Tracey speaks to us. It's normally short and I'd like to say it is always to the point but some of the most memorable coach chats from her have involved some wacky metaphor! I remember once she was speaking to us about how we needed a strong performance. 'A house is strong, you mustn't let anyone up the garden path,' she said, and then finished off by saying something like how we had to put a roof on that house. I'm confused trying to explain it! Most of the time we got the gist though, and actually some of her team chats eased our nerves because they were so random and got a few giggles and smiles. And then the captain talks. Tracey and all the coaching staff leave the room and so it is just all the players and the captain, Ama. Ama always does something for us beforehand – whether it is giving us gifts or playing a silly game or doing some singing, there is always something she has planned that brings us together. This time she had some bits of paper with different letters on and we all had to put them together. She wanted us to put the bits of paper up on the wall and it ended up spelling out the sentence: 'This is us, why not now?'

Ama's message was motivating and it was a great way of momentarily forgetting about the enormity of what we were going to face. And then we stepped out on court and that was it. The biggest thing for me was that I knew it wouldn't be as hard as playing against Jamaica. Jamaica was a tough bloody game and they have always been our bogey team. I think I sort of knew that nothing would be as tough as that game. And of course I knew the Australian players fairly well. I knew the combination I was coming up against – hell, I knew the goal shooter I was coming up against; I had just won a premiership with her. It was my teammate

Caitlin Bassett. She was the Diamonds captain, a good friend and someone I knew very well. They mixed the goal attack around as well and at one point the GA who came on was the GA for Lightning so I was playing against a combination I train against week in, week out.

I had forgotten about a training session that Noeline had put on at the beginning of the year. As Caitlin and I greeted each other on court, the memory flashed back into my head. Noels had organised some sessions for just Bass and myself, one-on-one in the circle. She knew we both were trying to better ourselves for Lightning and when she set us up on that training court we knew it was going to be one hell of a battle!

The thing between Bass and me was that we didn't hold back. We knew that if we made each other better here, in training as teammates, we'd both be even better in the Com Games. It was all about challenging ourselves to find new ways to beat each other in training, knowing that we'd most probably meet each other in Com Games at some point and we'd go head-to-head where there was no holding back. We laid bare our strength and weaknesses in training because when it came to a game that mattered, we both had to find a way to be the better player.

To the final. I was reading the ball, I was connecting well with my GD and outside defenders, I was getting my finger-tips on balls, I was getting turnovers and intercepts. We were clicking as a unit. We did the usual, we played our normal game. Eboni started at GD and then switched up at half-time and Ama came on. The momentum was swinging both ways; it was goal for goal all the way through. It was an exciting game all right, not just for the crowd watching in the stadium but for all the people watching on TV. This was one of the last sports to have its medal-decider matches, so anyone who tuned in hoping to catch a last bit of action from the Com Games was in for a treat! The problem with having played in the game, not watched it, is that things are all muddled into one in my memory. I don't remember what happened our end, I just remember that I think we were down by about four goals in the last quarter. And then we brought ourselves back level . . . and then those final few seconds.

'Really, Geev? Netball? Really?!' A flashback of my mum's voice came into my head, clear and crisp as if it was yesterday, as I watched what was happening down the other end of the court. I was right up to my third-line, I was leaning forward as far as I could and I could barely breathe with excitement. We were level with Australia now: the score was 51–51. The seconds were ticking by, the ball had just been down our end and all I could think about was that conversation I had had with my mum years ago and the confused look she gave me when I told her about this new sport I had fallen in love with.

I watched Jo, our champion goal shooter, as she took her shot. The ball rose into the air . . . and missed the goal. This was it now. It was over. And then Helen got the rebound

. . . Oh! Yes! We have another shot at goal! She missed. The klaxon had sounded, there was no time left to go – Then the whistle blew. Obstruction called! What? I couldn't hear the roar of the crowd or the screams from the spectators over the thumping in my chest. Time seemed to stand still.

And then another voice came into my head: 'We need you to make up numbers, Gee, can you stand at the back and wave your arms around and jump a bit?' My best friend from school. The conversation we had years ago, the reason I was here, the reason I was standing, barely able to breathe, as I watched Helen take the shot to goal that was to win us gold in Australia, against Australia.

It all seemed to be happening in slow motion as the ball went up, went over and . . . fell cleanly through the net. Goal! My brain needed time to process what had happened . . . the goal. The shot went in. OK, we'd won, right? We had won? No . . . I looked up to the scoreboard, was that right, was I reading it right? Fifty-two England . . . we'd won, we'd won, WE'D BLOODY WON! Hell, yeah! A shiver of pure adrenaline, excitement, euphoria . . . call it what you will, it felt like there was electricity running through me and I exploded into a scream of pure joy.

There aren't many moments in my life that I can remember in such vivid detail but I can honestly say, that Commonwealth Games on the Gold Coast when we were tied with Australia until the final few seconds of the game – I think I will have that moment tucked away somewhere safe in my mind for ever. And when I'm old and grey and can't remember what day it is, I will close my eyes and hear with crystal clarity the squeaks of my trainers on that polished court, the way the ball felt in my fingertips, the smell of my newly made England dress and the joy of knowing that after years and years of training and playing and competing and losing, we had struck gold.

I ran to my teammates. We were jumping and hugging. There were hugs and tears then there were people running on court from all over and there were pile-ons, and it was just a moment I wouldn't ever forget. When you have all that celebrating together on court, you forget all the people in the crowd. I was lying on the floor and everyone was on top of me screaming and shouting and crying and I turned my head to look at the crowd. I wanted to celebrate with our fans too. And when I got up I saw my brother and my mum hugging and Mum just had the biggest, proudest smile on her face. It was the first time she had stayed for an entire game in a big competition. It was a momentous occasion in many ways! I did say to her afterwards that I was surprised she stayed in for this one and she just said to me, 'You know what, I was just content you guys had got yourself in a position to contend. You had given yourselves a chance for a gold medal and you gave the Aussies a contest they will never forget!' She believed we could do it, and that was the difference. That belief. We had it too. It's just such a euphoric moment. You get flashbacks of when you first played the game, and previous games and training, and then, finally, you get that feeling that you have managed to achieve something that you have wanted for so long.

Whenever I watch a game on TV, and it doesn't matter what sport it is, any team game, I always like to watch the footage of the winning team and the losing team. I like to see how different players deal with the emotions and their reactions to either winning or losing. And I did that then on court. I knew what losing was like, I've been there.

All the time the game is going on, you are in battle mode. For sixty minutes it is you against them. But when that final whistle goes, that's it and there is nothing but respect for the other team – in this case, the losing team. I went around court and saw my past teammates, my current team-mates, my good friends, and I wanted to shake all of their hands. It is something you do in netball to finish the game off and it's about respecting your opponents because you recognise the heart and soul they put into the game, just as you did. Then you go back to your team and celebrate. It could have gone either way and that is what made it so emotional. I've been in games before and you've been up by five or six or ten goals and you know it's in the bag. But that game, no one knew. There was tremendous heartbreak for the Aussies because they lost it in that final few seconds, and tremendous excitement for us because we won it in those dying few seconds.

The crowd were on the edge of their seats right until the end, but once that final whistle went the Australian fans went very quiet and left very quickly! I remember being a bit shocked. I knew everyone had been hoping for an England vs Australia final ever since we beat Jamaica; they were gunning for it as it was a guaranteed medal for them. And gold at that; they pretty much thought it was theirs for the taking. 'Come on, guys, just appreciate the game!' I thought, but the fans were too upset to stay. They were in shock. And so were we! The medal presentation was a bit of a blur but I remember as soon as the England flag went up we were all in floods of tears. The England team were the last to walk out for the presentation; the Jamaicans came out first, happy and dancing in third place. Then the Australian team walked out sombrely before we made our way excitedly to the podium. Mum said she overheard someone describing the Australian team walk-out as looking like they were going to work on Monday morning and ours as looking like we were leaving work on Friday afternoon!

By the time we got back to the changing rooms we were a little bit giddy with adrenaline and excitement. There was more laughing and tears and joking and someone said, 'Remember our conversation in Sydney?!' From a team in despair after a thirty-five-goal loss to a club side to beating the world number-one netball team! Our CEO Jo Adams came in and congratulated us and she said, 'Oh my God, is there anything I can get for you girls? You don't know what you've just done for netball, for England Netball, please tell me if there is something I can do for you!' And I was the cheeky one in the corner and shouted out, 'BONUS!' And then everyone shouted at the same time, 'BONUS!' We don't get paid much as athletes; we get £1,000 for playing in the Com Games, we get nothing else for finishing with a medal or winning it. I think in the end she gave everyone an extra £2,000 each, which was amazing. OK, it's nothing in terms of what footballers get but, still, it was something else to celebrate!

Jo told us that the gold medal had made her job and her team's job a lot easier. It meant they could secure for England Netball some future funding. We had known for three or four years that Sport England had said they would stop all funding for England Netball in 2019, so that wasn't a shock for us. The shock came when Sport England decided to reverse that decision and continue the funding until 2022. This was the only time that they had changed their minds. So what we had achieved just then, and over the past year, helped everyone notice us. England Netball had proved they were worth the investment and to have Sports England turn a decision round, for the first time in history, and say, 'You know what, we are going to stick around and continue supporting you, we can see what brilliant work you do. We want to see more success with England Netball and we know that can happen' – well, that was probably worth more than any gold medal.

When I read about the number of women taking up netball now my heart swells with pride. There has been a 44 per cent increase in participation in the twelve months since we won gold and it is the UK's number-one female participation sport. What a legacy that is, what a time to be involved in the game, knowing that future generations of girls have a sport that has such a positive and powerful impact. The netball court is our safe space and our chance to get together and show what a formidable force a team of women can be.

13 THE ROCK
OF THE ROSES

'At the end of the day, it's a game of netball, no one has died.'
Noeline Taurua

LACHLAN had come to see some of our Com Games; in fact, he even came to the grand final. It was a bit weird afterwards. I went up to him and thanked him for being there but it was very awkward. There was no love any more, but no real hatred or anger either, it was just a very weird feeling. Mum, give her her dues, made sure she involved him with our family and friends at the event but he didn't want a part of that. He didn't want to sit with any of them and I'm sad to say it did put a bit of a damper on our victory. I think I was affected by him being there more than I thought I would be. He drove back to the Sunshine Coast that night and that was it. I think I only saw him once more after that. I can't tell you for certain why he came to the Games. Perhaps he felt some sort of strange obligation to be there? He loved going to sporting events and, as a PE teacher, loved watching rugby, gymnastics and athletics, so he probably didn't want to give up a ticket. He knew a lot of the Australian netball girls when I played with them in the league and probably, like most Australians, expected them to win. I can't say I am sorry to have disappointed him.

After the final, I went to New Zealand for a week with my brother and it was just what the doctor ordered. Noels had given me the week off as a chance to take a break and get myself fresh again for the start of the new Suncorp Super Netball season. Raoul and I spent the week horse-riding with our cousins, spending some quality time together, chilling. It was just perfect and I felt so refreshed afterwards.

Bizarrely, though, I found myself really missing my England team. Half of the squad were now playing out in the league for Australian teams while the other half were still involved in the English Netball Superleague. The ones who were in Oz managed a bit of a break, did some travelling, took a week or so to chill, while the other six – Jade, Beth, Jodie, Eboni, Kadeen and Natalie – flew back to the UK.

They got a huge welcome when they arrived back in London; there were flowers for them, lots of media interest. Lots of fans who had set their alarms to watch us in the final were there cheering for them. It was unreal! It was brilliant to see those girls being in the papers and on the internet and you'd turn round and BBC Sport would be interviewing them and then Sky Sports were interviewing them – they were everywhere! Then there was us, left in Australia feeling a bit left out, back to business with pre-season training with no one making a fuss of us!

I really wanted us to be all together, I guess. It had been such an intense couple of weeks and we had gone through so much. I normally quite like the break afterwards, but this time I missed them.

And the girls in England were all being treated like stars (rightly so, of course). They had invites to this, invites to that – they got asked to go to the BAFTAs! Everyone wanted to speak to them, to have photos with them. They said it was incredible. There was so much interest from the media too – they were on breakfast TV, lunchtime shows, radio shows, they did newspaper interviews . . . and meanwhile back in Australia, well, I probably don't need to say it was the exact opposite!

The biggest problem was obviously that we had beaten Australia on their home turf. No one could give a crap about congratulating us! I went back home to the Sunny Coast and my beautiful medal just sat there in my bedroom. The girls back in the UK were wearing their medals out all the time, in every interview they did, when they did appearances at schools, when they visited community centres or did talks at the local netball clubs – I was honestly a little envious; I wanted to wear my medal too and show it off at all these events! It was definitely a tale of two teams. There wasn't much that came of it all for those of us who were playing out in Australia. I even said to my management company, 'Surely this is the perfect opportunity to be creating more revenue for me with some sort of sponsorship deal or something? Surely someone wants to jump on the bandwagon, this doesn't come around often and, in my case, it's been twenty years in the making!' but there was just nothing.

Anyway, there was no time to dwell. I had the next season with Lightning to focus on, and as Noeline had given me that one week off to recharge I was left with only one week to train with the team before the season started. Two weeks since we won the Commonwealth Games and it was time to be back in action in the league. I hit the ground running and, as I was captain again, I had to fly to Sydney for official launch day with the captains of the other league teams. At one point, when the microphone came to me, I was asked, 'As reigning premiers, do the Lightning have what it takes to get another win and be back-to-back champions?' There was definitely an air of increased rivalry between the teams – we were the hunted this year and everyone wanted to bring us down.

I do remember there being quite a sting from the Australian head coach, Lisa Alexander, who was quoted as saying that the inclusion of international players in the Australian domestic league wasn't having a positive impact on the national team. 'I can't say it any other way, I'm the national coach and this [English players in Super Netball] has clearly assisted them to win this gold medal. That's our high-performance system working for another country.' Ouch! But how funny. All those years ago when I was not allowed to play in the Australian league and represent England because England didn't think it was right. But I knew deep down that it was only going to benefit my career and my netball ability. And now Australia are cross that we have become too good!

As Lightning were reigning champions, I wanted to lead us off to a great start again. Our first game was against Giants, who we had beaten in the grand final at the end of last season. It was a tricky game for us; everyone was touting it as the 'grand final rematch', and we lost. It wasn't a heavy loss, there was just a three-goal difference, but everyone was probably a bit flat to begin with. Our attacking end featured Caitlin Bassett and Steph Wood – the Australian Diamond combination – and they were coming off the defeat from Com Games. And myself and Karla, who had played in the defensive circle, had also been through the hype of the Games so I don't know if that played a bit of a part too. I think we were all just a little bit knackered.

It was a tough game to kick off the league and our next two games were equally tight and resulted in us losing. We didn't panic. We had to keep our circle quite tight, we had to keep each other focused as in the community there were a few mumbles. People were now touting us as 'one-hit wonders'. And there was definitely a bit of angst. We were 0–3 down at the start of the 2018 season but losing by small margins (I think it was 2–2 goals or something like that). So it wasn't an ideal start, but we didn't give up. We tried to keep everything very tight and very positive. We also had a great performance analyst, Anthony Bedford, who was able to give us a plan for what it would take to still make the top four. Having a plan like that, having evidence in front of us that all was not lost, helped boost our confidence and reassured us that we were still on track.

There is such a fantastic community vibe on the Sunshine Coast but it is a group of small towns and, while they really got behind us and the success we had in 2017, there was an air of doubt creeping in after those first few defeats. We had a brilliant media following on the coast, which meant that every loss was played out across the radio and TV, and as the losses clocked up, it was very important to us to stay quite positive and realistic in our comments. We got some wins and we kept ourselves in contention and things took on a more positive stance in the community – everyone started to have faith in us again!

We hit a bit of a rocky patch when Noeline lost her father. She went back to New Zealand for a couple of weeks, as she was to lead the funeral ceremonies and they went on for a week because her father was fairly high up in the Maori community. That was tough for the whole team. Our manager also lost her ex-husband who she was still very close to, and of course my marriage was broken and I was going through the process of divorce proceedings, so you could say we had a few serious personal problems in the team. But what we managed to do well as a team was enjoy each other's company and have fun and leave whatever was going on personally at the door. 'At the end of the day, it's a game of netball, we're not going to die out there,' was Noels's favourite quote to us. We just needed to appreciate what we had, appreciate life, and realise that at the end of the day it's just a game.

Halfway through the season and there was talk about girls signing up for next year and who would be staying on in the club. I made sure that all the girls were getting things they had been promised, that everyone was happy with what they were doing. I wanted to ensure that we could look after each individual player and their personal circumstances. Then it came to me talking to my manager and the CEO. They said, 'You're not getting any younger. We were going to offer you a one-year contract but, after talking to your manager, we will give you two.' I was taken aback. I ask you, is that any way to make a player feel valued? Feel wanted? Let alone the fact that I had captained their side to victory in their debut season and this season we were picking ourselves up nicely? I was pretty shocked and slightly sad. I would have thought the conversation could have gone something like this: 'We appreciate everything you have done for the club, Geva. You have backed it up with performance and, taking into consideration your age, we'd like to offer you a two-year deal.' Now to me, that's fair. I was also aware that Noels was under contract with

Lightning for one more year and I would want at least another two. Would I want to play under another coach if she wasn't there for my second year?

I started to look around. I think I thought perhaps it was time to move out of my comfort zone. Try to bring something else to my game, surround myself with new people, push myself a bit – all these things were going through my mind as the season continued. I was genuinely knocked a bit after that first conversation with the CEO. I guess I was probably a bit slower the first couple of games into the season, but I think we all were. We were all a bit lethargic, particularly the internationals who had played in the Com Games. But as the season progressed, I found my rhythm again and Karla and I ended up being a great defensive combination, with me getting the most deflections that year and ending up high on the list for the most defensive rebounds and intercepts. It showed that I had found my form, that I was still strong. I put all thoughts about a move to the back of my mind; there were no decisions that had to be made until the end of the season and I wanted to be able to focus on what I was doing now as captain.

The season was still going OK for us, but the big blessing came with a new rule that was brought in, the bonus point rule. In essence it was this – when you win, you get five points, but the new rules meant you could also get a point for every quarter you won throughout the game. Basically you were rewarded even if you lost a match. We were against it. This was changing the sport, the whole thing, we said.

Whereas before you'd go through a netball game like this: find your feet in the first and second quarter, the third quarter would be your championship quarter, and the fourth quarter you bring home the win. Now, you are wanting to win every bloody quarter because there is a point up for grabs! In fairness, it made the competition quite exciting and, after initially being so dead against it, we found that it actually worked out well for us. We had won pretty much the most quarters against every team, so even though we lost matches we were still getting points, which was putting us in contention for a final-four spot on the table. It pissed a lot of people off because we lost more games but had more points. You, as the losing team, could still get three points and the winning team five points. There wasn't much in it. Each team started to cheer on drawn quarters where neither team got any points.

We played Vixens in Melbourne and beat them, which secured us fourth spot on the table. We had a shocker in one of our quarters; we could have ended up finishing third, which meant we could have hosted the final, but we ended up finishing fourth and we had to go down to Brisbane and play the Firebirds, who'd finished third, in the knockout final. Straight after the Vixens game I came off and I was asked about what I thought about our next game, against the Firebirds. I was quite honest. I hadn't thought too much about what I was going to say, so when they asked me about it, I said it would be a great contest, that the team had some real firepower across the court and that there was a great state rivalry growing between our two teams. The match was set to be a cracker, I said. As the journalist quizzed me some more, I got a bit more heated and continued the interview by saying I found it very disrespectful that the Firebirds hadn't acknowledged us as another team in Queensland. We were teams from the same state and yet we were largely ignored. We were providing another pathway for girls to come into elite netball . . . I think I started to rant.

These feelings had been building up all season; as captain I am obviously privy to quite a lot of information, and I felt that some of the decisions that the Firebirds made were a deliberate dig at us and that they wanted us to play second fiddle to them. They had their season launch in Mooloolaba, which is our home town on the Sunshine Coast. They had their clinics up around there, our home area, and they had a slogan that said, 'Queensland is a one-team state'. I just found it so disrespectful and I decided not to hold my tongue any more and just speak quite fairly and honestly. We all felt that we weren't getting any respect from our fellow Queensland teams and it just put even more fire in our bellies to win. Enough was enough.

It was just funny as it got picked up massively in the media as this big story and they said that I had issued a 'war-cry!' The next day the CEO of Netball Queensland, Catherine Clark, felt she had to issue a public response, something meaningless like, 'If Geva wants to sit down and discuss things . . .' That was even funnier. Our CEO pulled me into the office and was not happy. She told me quite frankly, 'This is not how we operate, Geva!' But I wasn't backing down. 'To be honest, Danielle,' I replied, 'I am standing up for this team, something we should have done a long time ago.' Yes, I was on my soapbox, but I'd had some really nice messages from Melbourne Storm, the NRL team in Melbourne and our owners, as well as the University of the Sunshine Coast. They backed me up 100 per cent; they were happy to get more people fired up over netball, more bums on seats – although they did also say to me that I had to back it up next week when we played Firebirds in the semi-final! Still, I had support from the right people and that's what mattered.

The week before this monumental match was tough. There was a lot of media interest, lots of reporters wanting more comments from me to fuel the fire even more. We travelled down to Brisbane, to the Firebirds' home ground, and straight away we knew it was going to be a feisty atmosphere. Eighty per cent of the spectators were Firebird fans – it was their home turf, after all.

They had this beer tent right behind the posts that had a whole load of drunks in shouting 'Queensland! Firebirds!' every time our shooters were down that end. But you know what? Our fans, our minimal 20 per cent share of the spectators, completely and utterly blew away the whole stadium. They overpowered the Firebird supporters and everyone was amazed at this level of noise and support from such a small group and it was just brilliant. Our fans were the eighth player in that match and they got us over the line. We ended up winning that match by one goal, 57–56, after being down earlier in the last quarter and it was just crazy. That was the hardest game of the final three games we played but it gave us such momentum as a team. I had 'talked the talk', as it were, and we definitely showed the opposition that they needed to show us some respect. That win gave us strength as a team and it was the crowd that won it for us. We were so thankful to them. We made sure that in every interview afterwards we thanked them and praised them. So many of them decided that if we won the week after they would fly to Perth for the grand final! But first we had another hurdle in the way and a job to do, which was to head to Sydney and play in the semi-final against the Giants. It was a tough game against them – they had a couple of girls who were retiring at the end of the season and were playing with a lot of heart – but we just hit the ground running and we felt a little bit unstoppable. It turned out we were! We won. We beat the Giants in Sydney to book us a ticket through to our second grand final and to have the opportunity to defend our title. After a fairly slow and unthreatening start to the season, in only our second season as a club here we were again, in our second consecutive grand final.

Lightning were happy for me to delay my decision about signing a new contract until after the final. I needed to give that all my focus and concentration and I appreciated the leeway. The final was a tough, well-fought battle with West

Coast Fever and one hell of a win – for us! We had won back-to-back titles in our two-year history and it was just the most magical, crazy and exciting end to the season. I was physically and emotionally exhausted and I think I was ready for a change.

After the grand final we had a week before we had our farewell gala dinner and I still hadn't decided about where I was going to go. The gala dinner was on the Friday and I told Lightning that I'd take the weekend to think things over. We had achieved something so special as a team and there was a big part of me that thought, 'Do I want to stay and keep that momentum going?' Equally, if we had lost the final, I might have had a burning urge to stay behind and rectify things, chasing that title win again. So that weekend, knowing I had to give my decision on Monday, was full of honest conversations with Mum and my manager. I was sought after, which was nice; there were a few teams interested in me. It was a case of working out what would be best for me and for now. I started to put myself a little higher up the list now; I was starting to put plans in place for my life once my elite playing career was over. First and foremost I wanted to make sure I finished my university degree. I am so passionate about teaching. I want to be able to give something back, to make a difference. I have seen how great coaches and great teachers can make a difference in a child's life and I have seen how poor ones can kill a dream before it has even started. I want to use what I have learned in my playing career and make sure I am the sort of teacher who can ignite a passion in a child. It will be incredible to inspire students to learn, to push themselves, to have a dream and go for it. With teaching, you have the potential to shape young people's minds, the potential to show them the world we live in and provide them with tools so they can go out into that world and flourish. I like the idea of working as a team in a school, in a faculty with like-minded teachers in an environment where we are all striving towards the same goal: to provide a great education for the next generation. And I guess, from a personal point of view, I want to be able to be the first person in my immediate family to get a university degree. I know I won't be playing elite netball for ever, so teaching will be my next challenge and, like with everything I do, I want to feel fulfilled and do that to the best of my ability.

Leaving Lightning was an unbelievably tough decision and not one single factor was the cause of me leaving. I loved the community, I loved the beaches, the lifestyle, I loved walking into the local shops and people wanting to talk to me and hug me. After my move became public knowledge I was in the post office and two ladies came over to me and gave me a hug and said they were going to miss me. A guy came and shook my hand. They made you feel like little rock stars – everyone knew who you were, they always wanted to talk or say well done, or tell you what they thought about how a particular game went. I will definitely miss that sense of support from the Sunshine

Coast community as they were a massive reason behind our success.

But I wanted a change and a new challenge. In leading the team to two successive victories I felt like I had done all that was asked of me by the club. I had also just been named Goal Keeper of the Year again at the Netball Australia awards evening. I remember going out with the whole team for brunch and Bass and another player, Kelsey, told us all that they would be moving on. I hadn't signed anywhere else yet but I was seriously considering things. It was quite an emotional catch-up as we had gone through a lot together, but I think we all appreciated that we needed to focus on us as individuals now and things were pulling us in different directions for a variety of reasons.

So, where to go? I have always gone to teams where I feel I have something to offer, where I can develop that team in some way. I take the greatest reward in bringing a team together, pushing them forward, making a difference. I had made another decision during the season and changed management, moving from TLA; they had been great but – perhaps because they had a growing amount of talent on their books and I was quite isolated on the Sunshine Coast – I wasn't getting a lot of action. We parted company on good terms and I put my playing career in Trent Tavoletti's capable hands. I'd actually had a fair bit to do with him over the last couple of years, as he helped make sure any English girls who were playing down under got fair contracts and he had used me as a sounding board. Trent came back to me and was embarrassed by the offer that Lightning had put on the table compared to what he was getting from elsewhere and, in the end, we narrowed it down to two clubs. And my final decision went in favour of Collingwood Magpies in Melbourne.

The important thing for me was that I wasn't leaving Lightning on a bad note. I still respect the team and the coaches and I am proud to have been part of the inaugural set-up and to have brought them success two years running. I don't know what it will be like going back there and playing my first game against them, but so far I've felt nothing but love and support from the community.

It was time to put myself first. I'd had a pretty shit time in my personal life for the past eighteen months or so, but on the flip side I'd probably had the best eighteen months of my netball life. Winning back-to-back Premierships, the Com Games, being named Best Player in the World twice. As the shit was hitting the fan in my personal life, as my marriage came to an end, I'd been able to focus on my game and play the best netball I have ever played. Maybe having nothing to look forward to in my life except netball, nothing to focus on but putting my heart and soul into the court, was the reason for this success. Some players lose a bit of focus once they become married because there is something else to think about: their husband, children . . . I am not saying that doesn't happen to sportsmen as well, but it has been my experience of playing with women who start a family. I had nothing, so I put everything into my netball. There is probably a message somewhere here, something like, shit does happen but that doesn't mean everything is shit. You can't always let failure in one small part of your life overshadow the great things you have achieved and will achieve. Sometimes the failures help to shape you to be the person you are now, and failing in one area doesn't mean you give up on everything. There aren't many things I regret in my life but, yes, getting married is one. I will probably always regret it as deep down I knew it wasn't the right decision for me and I should have stopped the relationship sooner. I am sad that I wasted all those years with someone who in the end didn't make me happy. So I focus now on making myself happy.

Having gone with my gut, I left Sunny Coast and moved back down to Melbourne, to a fresh start, a new club. I love it there. I have a good friendship base, plus my brother is there with his godfather and family. Everything had fallen back into place after me being in limbo for months, perhaps even years. I now have a place to call home again. The fact that I can live with my brother without angst is amazing; he is my rock. And work is amazing too. It was fantastic to come to Collingwood. You can rock up there at seven in the morning and you've got the training all under one roof whether it's on court, in the gym, altitude training, recovery or the track outside. And you have all the physicians, physios, welfare staff, nutritional experts – anyone you could possibly want. It is an amazing set-up.

Collingwood have been around for 127 years, first as a football club and the netball club was formed in 2017. They are the club that everyone loves to hate. I think back in the day they were very arrogant, very vocal, very big-headed, and it was all about winning. But that culture has shifted in the past couple of years and they are making changes. Their mantra 'Humble in victory, gracious in defeat' is helping them focus on the right attitude. And the people who work there are good people. I haven't grown up with the AFL or Aussie Rules culture of just being involved in one team your whole life, but people here have and they are passionate about Collingwood, even if that passion is sometimes misdirected. I was looking forward to coming to the club and joining the netball team.

I knew a bit of their history too. Over the last two years the team had bought so many different players they pretty much had most of the Australian Diamonds line-up. Everyone picked them as the 'dream team' in that first year of the Suncorp Super Netball League set-up. But they came in fourth that year and didn't make finals the following year. It's that classic saying: they are a 'team of champions rather than a champion team'. I don't necessarily want to come in and play for the best club, the club at the top; I want to come in and work hard, work on bringing the team success and hitting milestones together. We'll focus on short-term challenges first, like winning the derby battle against the other team in Melbourne (my old team, Vixens) and then perhaps focus on finishing in the top four. I am not saying I can change everything myself but I will keep my professional standards high, let my play do the talking and, more importantly, relax and enjoy playing. We have a road to travel as a team and it's important to remember why we play – we enjoy the game. The focus needs to go back on that rather than on getting wins all the time. We have to remember that we are not going to be doing this for ever – some of us might have another ten years, some of us might retire in a year – but netball will continue long after we are gone and forgotten so it's important to enjoy the moment. Right now we have a common goal. We know it will be bloody hard work and some things might not go to plan, but we can keep putting our best foot forward and keep having fun while we are doing it.

Joining Magpies has brought about a new start for me professionally and personally. Funnily enough, before joining Magpies was ever a thought in my mind, I met a guy who plays for the football club there, and his story is pretty similar to mine. He is American and had just completed a mechanical engineering degree when he got scouted and asked to try out for AFL. He came over, they liked him, and he's been involved with the club for the last four years. He is six foot eleven, the same height as my brother, and we have been dating for the last six or seven months. In the early days when there was talk of me joining the club he wanted to make sure the decision to move to Magpies wasn't anything to do with him. I reassured him that it wasn't, that it was all about me and what was best for me professionally. But I won't lie, it has worked out quite nicely that we are at the same club! We go in to work in the mornings together, we see each other during the day. We are both new to the country but we both love Australia. Yes, he has met my mum. The final test will be Dad but for now it's pretty cool getting to know someone new, being able to open myself up emotionally again. Don't get me wrong, it is daunting and my self-confidence is taking time to build up again, but we are taking things nice and slowly. I'm happy. And that is all I can ask for.

14 AND THE
WINNERS ARE . . .

'Just play. Have fun. Enjoy the game.' Michael Jordan

T HE end of 2018 was still so full on with travel plans, work plans, international duties – and retrieving some of my belongings. To cut a long story short, my ex-husband still has a lot of my personal stuff, things that are of no monetary value or use to him but that are sentimental items and mean a lot to me. I was due to head off on my travels, for some much-needed R&R in America and Canada and then some netball work in Singapore. Then I would be heading back to the UK for a couple of awards evenings and England training camps.

But before that, after the season had finished, I also squeezed in a trip with Raoul to Thursday Island, which is located north of Queensland. We took small planes, drove bumpy roads, and even flew out in a helicopter to meet the locals and deliver coaching sessions. It was a great way to explore more of this beautiful country, to inspire and hopefully empower the locals, and for us to appreciate the history and culture and achievements of Aboriginal Australians and Torres Strait Islanders across the country. Raoul and I loved it.

I was back in Melbourne for a few days before I flew out to begin my travel adventures in America. My holiday was broken up with a visit to Singapore, where I was running a netball clinic with Netball Singapore. I love these clinics; it's a chance to meet and run sessions for young players and their coaches and it's quite rare that I find the time to be able to deliver such sessions, although I'd love to do more. Then it was time to fly back to England and I was able to spend a night in Bournemouth before I was due to attend my first event as a gold medal winner at the *Sunday Times* Sportswomen of the Year Awards.

The ceremony was held at the News UK offices in London Bridge and I was excited – not only would I be catching up with the girls, but I had brought along my new man and I wanted to show him the cool landmarks of London. When we arrived at the venue his first comment was one of shock: 'Why is it so small?! Is this the right room?' He couldn't get over that if this was celebrating the top women players in sport why wasn't it full to the brim. At Collingwood, we go to awards as a club and the rooms are filled with hundreds of people – ten people or more sit round each massive table, and there are probably over sixty tables. This event had roughly thirty tables in total, with six or eight people on each. 'If this is meant to be the best of British . . .' he said, looking at me, smiling.

It was great to be able to go there, though; although I call Australia home now, I'm still very proud to represent England and it was exciting to have been nominated in the Team of the Year category, alongside the British wheelchair basketball team, Chelsea Football Club and Team GB's 4x100-metre relay team. I was there with our captain Ama Agbeze, Jo Harten, Helen Housby and Tracey, plus our CEO Jo Adams, and it was a real honour to be in that room. Being based in Australia, I miss so much of what is happening in British sport. You just get Australian athletes and Australian sport shoved down your neck, you don't get to see much of what is happening in the rest of the world. So it was brilliant to see and hear so much about what was happening in women's sports in the UK.

It was incredible, the list of triumphs and successes that were talked about that evening. It might have been an intimate event in size, but it certainly packed a punch in showcasing the achievements of women's sport. There were a lot of people I wanted to see. Mum told me that she had put forward a nomination in the Inspiration category for her good friend Pat Mathie, who had come to watch me play when I first got picked for the England squad. She is an amazing woman who has done so much for sport where we lived when I was growing up. Her kids used to trampoline with us and she had set up a gymnastics club down in Bournemouth twenty-five years ago. It was brilliant to see her. And there was another woman, Georgia Hall, who won the Women's Golf Open as a junior. She is also a Bournemouth girl and I was very excited to meet her. You see, I'm not just England proud, I'm Bournemouth proud – you can take the girl out of Bournemouth but not Bournemouth out of the girl. Yes, I actually own one of those T-shirts!

The room was full of amazing sports stars, faces that you had seen on TV or in the papers, and I was a bit like, 'OMG, is that who I think it is?' Jessica Ennis-Hill was there, Dina Asher-Smith . . . and everyone looked so beautiful! I guess it is a nice change for us athletes – you're normally in your sports kit, hair pinned back, doing your job, so getting the chance to dress up was fun. Why not go to town! When it was announced we had won in our category we all went up on stage and I think we eclipsed the backdrop, being so tall and there being so many of us! That award meant a lot as it was voted by the *Sunday Times* readers, which meant that people were enjoying netball, they were enjoying what we were doing. We heard that night that six months after we had won gold at the Commonwealth, a survey commissioned by England Netball showed that over 130,000 adult women had started playing netball. And 77 per cent of adults who watched us at the Games said the Roses are an inspiration to young girls. Hearing those statistics is just mind-blowing. It makes our game feel so special – to inspire so many girls and adults alike is phenomenal. How can anything ever top that? Forget any medal or trophy or anything else: getting people active, getting more boys and girls on court, is our biggest achievement.

The Uganda series was coming up in December. I had been approached about taking the captaincy role for it a month or so before, as Ama was out with a knee injury. Of course, I was honoured to have been asked but I explained that I was struggling with personal matters and I actually needed special consideration to be excused from this series. I had so much stuff going on at home with my ex, getting my stuff back, trying to find a place to live in Melbourne, pack up my apartment and belongings on the Sunshine Coast and to relocate them to Melbourne in my car. My mind was all over the place. I didn't want to be captain unless I could give it my complete, undivided attention and effort. Tracey was initially not OK with the situation and I found this hard because I didn't want to leave my team in the lurch; however, I needed to get everything sorted. In the end we came to an understanding and Tracey gave me special consideration to miss that series. In turning down the captaincy role I potentially gave up the chance to lead England in the 2019 World Cup. Is it going to be a decision I regret? I don't think so. I can't do something without giving it my all and it wouldn't have been fair to do the job half-heartedly.

I trained with Collingwood for three weeks and then came back to England for Christmas. Having been out in Oz right after the Com Games and not able to be part of the team celebrations in England, I was really determined to attend the BBC Sports Personality of the Year Award and join all my teammates and revel in being nominated. We had been nominated for Team of the Year and Greatest Sporting Moment of the Year and whether we won or not, this was an opportunity I didn't want to miss.

I flew from Melbourne into Birmingham, where the awards were being held. I had been loaned a car by one of Mum's friends, Steve Hendy. He always gives me a set of wheels whenever I am in the UK and is an avid supporter of our sport. Mum drove the car up all the way from Bournemouth to Birmingham, picked me up from the airport and took me to the Holiday Inn she had booked just round the corner from the NEC. I had done a bit of online shopping before I left Australia and ordered three or four dresses from Dorothy Perkins and Boohoo, hoping that one of them would fit me (there is always a risk in ordering online when you aren't exactly a conventional body shape or height!). Thankfully, one of the dresses – just the one though! – was perfect. I spoke to some of the other girls from the team, who were in Loughborough getting ready for the awards. They were all having their hair and make-up done professionally before a coach would drive them down and I would meet them at the venue. I couldn't believe it – they were having professional make-up done and there was me who doesn't really wear make-up struggling to whack something on my own face!

I didn't have a lot of time to worry about it as Mum wanted to leave early so I could get there in plenty of time to soak up the atmosphere and enjoy the evening. The problem was, the traffic was bad, it was chucking it down with rain, and she got a bit lost. Instead of going left at a roundabout she ended up going all the way round and then out again and got herself in a bit of a tizz. I really wasn't worried about the detour, but she was very upset. 'No, Geva, it's not all right! I wanted to make this evening perfect for you!' Luckily one of us is less dramatic! I still arrived in plenty of time and met Tracey there. I was so pleased to see her – you know what it's like when you get to a party and you scan the room to try to see a familiar or friendly face, knowing there is strength in numbers!

The best thing about finding Tracey when I arrived was that I didn't have to walk the red carpet by myself. Talk about being a fish out of water! We both were and, I kid you not, the red carpet at these awards is like the one you see on TV at the Oscars. It was wide and long and there were TV camera crews, press, photographers all lined up along one side. The backdrop had all the sponsors' logos on it and Tracey and I started walking along, but we kept getting shouted at to stop and pose. It was so funny. We were like, how do we stand? What do I do with my legs? What should I do with my arms? We stood there trying to not look awkward and the photographers were just shouting at us to look this way and that way. I had one of my hands on my hip and was trying my hardest to pose effectively but how do you do that? No one teaches you that! I pull the worst face when I'm on the netball court but I don't care, I think screw it, it is what it is! But on the red carpet I just don't have a clue whether I should pout/smoulder/game-face it, so I just smiled and hoped for the best. I remember looking back at some of those photos of Tracey and me on the red carpet and it looks like we are holding hands! Our legs looked good though – we nailed the pose!

After a few minutes you are sort of ushered on as more personalities arrive and we thought we had made it to the end of the red carpet without being called across for a TV interview but then, at the last moment, someone grabbed us. A lady came over and asked if we'd spare a moment for a chat and we ended up speaking on TV, although I can't remember what the programme was. I was so jet-lagged and bewildered by this whole experience, I have no idea what I said! We finally made it to the end of the red carpet and went inside. The other girls were all late leaving Loughborough and didn't have time to enjoy that red-carpet experience, unfortunately – or maybe fortunately, considering the level of stress it can cause!

I probably spent the whole evening in a state of mouth-open excitement. When Tracey and I first walked in we met Billie Jean King and had a photo with her. Well, that was after we'd spent about five minutes saying to each other, 'Is it her? Is it her? Shall we go and say hi?!' Talk about setting the standard for the evening! The other girls met us before we all walked round to the stadium and it was just pure nuts. All these people are sat looking gorgeous and glamorous in this massive room and you want to look at everyone but not be obviously looking at everyone either. We have played in arenas like that, so the size itself isn't daunting – the daunting thing is trying to walk in heels when you are wearing a nice dress! We all ended up walking along the front row, right by the stage. We passed Lewis Hamilton and his family and Jessica Ennis-Hill, and then all of a sudden you notice all these cricketers and footballers and athletes who you have seen and supported on the TV and they are now just a few feet away. All the time we were all trying to be cool; I'd smile at people as we walked to our seats and I remember trying to see if I could spot Alistair Brownlee, but he wasn't there. We had a lot of people smile and watch us as we made our entrance, which, if you think about it, isn't that unusual as we were quite a sight to behold! Not only are we all so bloody tall, we've all worn heels and we are like these glamorous Amazonian women. Plus when we move, we move as one, so we made quite a noticeable entrance. So we were smiling at people, these super-athlete-stars, and they were smiling back and we were just having fun and soaking up the atmosphere and enjoying the company. We took our seats and the evening just turned out to be a really cool stage show with music and awards and interviews. We noticed that every time they were announcing the nominations for an award, someone from the TV team would alert the winners, who would then go backstage. Then when it was announced they had won they would come on stage for the interviews and to collect their gong. When it came to the Team of the Year award, we were a little, 'Oh we are still sat here, it can't be us . . . that's a pity.'

And then they announced we had won, and beaten the likes of the England football team. We were completely and utterly genuinely shocked! We couldn't believe it! I am sure I just shouted, 'Whattt?!' as I turned round to check I had heard right. Then we all had to slide out of our rows of seats, checking we hadn't got our dresses tucked in anywhere they shouldn't be, and then the next battle is you have to walk up the stairs in your heels! We all walked up as the auditorium just kept applauding and it was just an incredible feeling. To stand on the stage and look out at all the people who were clapping and then remember you are on live TV and there are thousands of people watching at home – it was beyond exciting. I don't think any one of us stopped smiling the whole time we were on stage and, fair play to Ama, she spoke beautifully on behalf of us all.

And then the strangest thing happened, Gabby Logan, the co-host, came over to us on stage and told us to wait. It was time for the Greatest Sporting Moment of the Year award. They started showing footage of the other nominated 'moments' and then it came to us and they showed in full the moment Helen scored the goal that was to win us Commonwealth gold. And the next thing we knew we had won that as well! The looks on our faces probably showed that we weren't expecting that award either; it was just the most amazing feeling and an amazing night. Greatest Sporting Moment is voted for by the public, which meant the world to us. It felt that our sport was being embraced by the country, and not only that, our most amazing moment was the voting public's most amazing moment as well. Winning that award felt like we had given our sport a whole new audience, and to be up on stage with the biggest names in the sporting world watching us and the fans at home supporting us, to be up there representing our country in a sport that was now getting the recognition it deserved – all in all it was an extraordinary night.

We went backstage after winning our second award as it had come to the end of the night and they were announcing the actual BBC Sports Personality Award. Then we got to stand on stage again with all the runners-up and winners and that was brilliant! We wanted photos, lots of photos, and netballers are so bossy (something that Harry Kane and Lewis Hamilton found out quite quickly!) – we organised everyone on stage for a series of shots.

I am a massive fan of Formula One so meeting Lewis was an insane moment for me! I made sure I wangled my way to the front and I had to touch him, so I put my hand on his shoulder . . . how corny am I?! But he was so cool, he didn't mind and the girls knew I was so happy to be within touching distance of him. Jo Harten and some of the other girls are massive football fans so they pretty much did the same with Harry Kane – it wasn't just me being embarrassing!

After the live show you all go back to where you first congregated in this big room and now they had filled it with food trucks with every conceivable type of food you could want to eat. There are lots of bars around the room too and everyone who came out of the auditorium was now ready to party! Everywhere you looked there were athletes of the most incredible calibre. Sporting stars in their prime, retired athletes, Olympians, Paralympians: the room was filled with legends. You feel very small and insignificant among all of them, knowing what they have done and achieved and worked hard to do, and will work hard carrying on doing. And what was more incredible was that so many of them came over to us and wanted to congratulate us! A lot of them told us that they had set alarms to watch our game at five in the morning and that was just mind-blowing.

We were a bit star-struck as all these big sports stars came over and then they would start chatting and we'd realise they were just normal like us. We had a great time! Stuart Broad the cricketer was one of the first over and spoke to us for ages, and then the CEO of Amazon UK came up and had a long chat. We spoke to the hockey girls, boxers, gymnasts. It wasn't just sportspeople; the Weasley brothers from the *Harry Potter* films, actors James and Oliver Phelps, came over to us and had a chat, which was super-cool. And I don't watch it but apparently there is a *Love Island* TV show or something in the UK? There were three of them there, a girl and two guys, and apparently they were the three that everyone loved. Only the London girls in our team knew who they were; I had no idea!

An hour or so into the evening a live band started and Clare Balding and all the hosts were first up on the dance-floor and started shouting over to us, 'Come on, girls!' And before we knew it they were dragging us on to the dance-floor like overexcited relatives at a wedding reception. It was so much fun! Apparently these awards are renowned for having a great after-party and this one certainly didn't disappoint. Everyone let their hair down and drank and ate whatever they wanted. Sometimes it can be hard to go to an awards evening when you are the only athlete or part of a small group of athletes there. You feel everyone is judging you on what you eat and whether you drink or not. But there was no judging here. Everyone was the same, everyone had the same appreciation for how bloody hard it was being an elite sportsman or sportswoman and we all just let our hair down. And took our shoes off! We aren't made for heels, us netballers, so our heels were off probably within the first hour and we were wandering around bare-foot – we had no shame!

The next day we all had to be in camp for England training. Spirits were definitely high all that week as we reminisced about that night. This was the last camp of 2018 and the end of an incredible year for the England netball team. A week later it was Christmas and so I went back to Mum's and we drove over to Holland to share the festivities with my brother, Dad and his family. It must be very hard for my mum and my dad's new wife and my hat goes off to both of them for the way they are able to accommodate us all with no angst or bad feelings. I have a lot of respect for that, the way they are content just to see all the children together. Myself and Raoul, Inez and Noor – we all get on so well. We love our dad and we love our mums and that quality time we spend together is so special. I appreciate it every time it happens because I know it can't be easy but it is done for our benefit. Those moments with family, that special bond we have . . . whenever I am finding things tough or get lonely, I remember that contentment I have when I am around my family. And one day, when I have a family of my own, it will become even more special.

The year 2018 was pretty amazing all things considered and it wasn't like I was aiming for anything in particular, I was just going about my business and whatever I was doing, I tried to do it well. There was something even more special about 2018 and I knew what it was at the beginning of December, but I wasn't allowed to mention it to anyone until the official announcement came through at the end of the month: I was to be awarded a CBE in the queen's New Year Honours list!

This is something I am struggling to get my head round. I still can't quite believe it. I am still in shock when people mention it and congratulate me – I know I probably sound like an authentic Aussie when I say something is 'unreal' but blimey, this was as unreal as it got!

I got the phone call when I was in Australia, a couple of days before I flew back to England. It was a call from the British Deputy High Commissioner in Canberra and the conversation (as I remember it because, let's be honest, it isn't an everyday sort of conversation and I was a bit blown away!) went like this: 'Geva, because of your services to netball, we'd like to present you with this CBE if you would accept it.' Of course, I said, 'Wow! Yes, please, thank you, yes thank you!'

She then continued to tell me that this was top secret and I wasn't allowed to tell my family until the announcement had been made public. Well, surely that is code for 'You can tell your mum!' I was actually at my boyfriend's place at the time and after I finished the conversation I was quite obviously in a state of shock. I had to tell someone! I told him, which was pretty safe as it turned out, because he didn't have a clue what a CBE was or why it was so special. He is American and he didn't give a crap, to put it nicely! I'm OK, I thought, I haven't broken any rules – he's not going to tell anyone. It literally went in one ear and out the other. The secret would be safe. But there was no way I wasn't going to tell Mum! So I rang her, and God knows what time it was in the morning, I think it must have been around 4 a.m., but she answered the phone right away. When I told her she pretty much lost the plot; her voice went up a couple of octaves and she was just so excited.

What I didn't realise at the time was that she had put in the application nominating me. She had been contacting people, from both across the netball spectrum and the charities I was involved with. She contacted England Netball for a reference but they told her they were thinking of putting forward some of the team themselves, including me. They wanted Mum to hand over all the letters and emails she had received in support of my application as they thought it would be better coming from a national governing body, but Mum decided against it. And it is thanks to her that I have been awarded my Commander of the British Empire award, as not a single other England netballer made the honours list.

Once I had got Mum to calm down I did try to hammer home that she had to keep this to herself and that I was breaking the rules by telling her. I did worry about her telling everyone as she gets so bloody excited about everything, but she did well and kept it to herself. And so did I. And as the end of December got closer we kept thinking, they must announce this soon. And then I started getting emails from Radio Solent and BBC South Today congratulating me and I knew that, at last, the good news was out. The Deputy High Commissioner had told me that it would be going to the media twelve hours before the official announcement so I knew that, now the likes of the BBC were contacting me, it was only a matter of hours before everyone knew!

* * *

When I woke up in the morning I had so many messages and texts from people in Australia and around the world. It was crazy. So I put out my 'thank you' post on social media and tried to respond to as many messages as I could. It still hasn't really sunk in; I still don't believe I am someone deserving of such an accolade. How can I be? I just do what I do, I play netball. I found all the attention and kind words and tributes overwhelming . . . Was it all real? I imagine that when I go to the palace, I will still think it's not real! I really hope that the Queen is there. Can you imagine how amazing that would be?! I adore the royal family. I am going to be in my element! And of course, I will take my mum and dad with me if I can. I would take everyone if I could, but we'll just have to wait and see. I might have to keep an eye on Mum if the Queen is there. I think I'll have to muzzle her – she's bound to say something she shouldn't or will go up and try to hug her or something!

EPILOGUE

*'I don't know where I'm going from here but I promise
it won't be boring.'*
David Bowie

I MET an old teammate, Johanna Haynes, from my Dorset
Junior days recently after playing for England at the
Copper Box arena at the beginning of 2019. It was a real
blast from the past; it seemed like only yesterday that Jo
and I, fresh-faced youngsters, were playing together and
now here she was watching me play with her seven-year-old
daughter Harriet. Harriet was really into netball, she told
me, and was playing at school, and I was struck by a sudden
instinctual longing in my heart. Mother and daughter,
watching netball together and playing netball together
. . . wouldn't that be wonderful? Maybe that will be me in
ten years' time, taking my own daughter to an England
match, telling her how I used to do it in my day or showing
her a trick or two on court.

Remember I mentioned the questions I am asked most

as an athlete? There is a new one doing the rounds just now – where do I see myself in ten years' time? – and that is precisely the image that comes to mind. We all dream about the future but generally don't give a picture to those dreams, and yet I saw Jo and Harriet and felt that actually, bringing children into the world, bringing a new generation into netball, sounds like a pretty cool dream. I know from experience that things don't always go to plan and you have to be open to change and not be too rigid in your planning. Ultimately I hope that in ten years' time I will be happy and I will be something I am proud of and making others proud – being the best daughter, best sister, best friend I can be. Teacher? Wife? Mother? Who knows, but I want to be happy with life because, at the end of the day, it's too short and all we actually eventually end up being is simply a memory for someone. I want to do my best to be a good one! My answer to the question at the moment is quite practical: 'still walking,' is my first response! My ankles are bloody terrible; I have no ligaments left in them now and I joke with the physios and say I just rely on my tendons (the tissue that connects muscle to bone). I suppose because I've had issues with my back and my knees, my ankles wanted a little bit of attention too. But I'll do what I have always done with my ankles – strap the hell out of them and carry on.

Travelling is also getting to be a factor in my life. I class Australia as my home and I miss it when I leave. I always feel unsettled flying over to the UK and excited about returning to Australia which makes me think I have found home. I have been travelling since I was very young, from Bournemouth to Bath, to training to trials, to this part of the country to that part . . . to Australia, to New Zealand . . . to all the amazing places I have been to with my netball. So perhaps in ten years' time I would like to be properly settled and answerable to just myself. Having been involved in netball from the age of sixteen means that I have been 'organised' all that time; all the decisions about training, where to train, how to train, have been made for me. All the decisions about where I need to be before a season starts, timings for this, checking in with someone, asking permission to do something or go somewhere . . . My whole life has been organised for me. Perhaps having control of my own diary might be nice in ten years. I want to be my own boss. As an athlete you are to a certain extent; you can control what you eat, how you train, the effort and intensity that you put in, and yet you are still under some sort of control. You are still answerable to someone because if you don't put in the effort and watch what you eat and you don't train and don't perform you have to explain why. I am older now and I probably work a bit harder in all the aspects of the game that I slacked in as a younger athlete.

I suspect a lot of people will probably retire after the World Cup in 2019. I'm not sure where I am at personally; I always thought maybe I would because I thought I would be married and possibly looking at starting a family, and I would concentrate on club netball and retire from the international scene. But now I am just going to see what happens. I definitely want a bit of a break after the World Cup; whether that means I have a break for a year or a couple of months I don't know yet. I definitely want to keep playing netball as long as I am still contributing to the team, as long as I still feel like I am an asset to a club and to my teammates. I want to do that for as long as possible.

In the short term I just want success at the World Cup, pure and simple. Australia are gunning for us now. We beat them in the dying seconds of a game that had their name all over it and that is their driving force, that is the fire in their belly. They want to come to our country and steal that medal back on our soil. People have realised we don't just talk the talk, we can put our money where our mouth is, but we are very conscious of trying not to get ahead of ourselves. That is something that we are reminded about as a team constantly – from the coach to the captain to the players – this isn't going to be easy. The World Cup won't be handed to us. We have put ourselves up there and now we have a big target on our back. All the other teams and countries playing want to win the World Cup and they want us to lose.

I am personally cautious about the New Zealand side. They have Noeline at the helm now, and Laura Langman as their captain. Along with Jamaica, they have some real firepower that hasn't been seen on the international scene for a while. It is setting up to be a fantastic World Cup and I really hope each team goes out there firing on all cylinders and giving it their all. If that is the case there will be some fantastic games for the fans. And I hope even more fans will get caught up in the excitement and edge-of-your-seat thrills that our game can provide. I was told just the other day by a lady who watched us play on TV at the beginning of the year that her son, who had never watched a netball game before, was glued to the telly. He told her that he thought it was better than football! How cool is that? Let's get that going, let's get everyone involved and behind us – boys, girls, mums, dads, grannies, uncles – enjoying the show. Because it is a show – a show that demonstrates dedication, teamwork, skill and perseverance. It's a game that shows nerves of steel and wills to win.

It's a game I'm bloody proud to be part of.

ACKNOWLEDGEMENTS

I WOULD like to dedicate this book to all those folk who have featured in my life thus far. From Lyn Gunson who spotted something in me in the early days, to Julie Hoornweg who had the balls to elevate me into the senior squad Noeline, you've showed me great empathy and put the fire back in my belly. My teachers from St Peter's, in particular Viv Hawkins and Patrick Lucas, who enlightened me with the balance of elite sport and education.

My oldest friends Vicky and Pete Simmonds, 'the twins' who know me better than most. To all my teammates that make me a better version of myself. Mo'onia Gerrard and Sonia Mkoloma, my besties who just get me.

To old love that has given me strength to stay true to myself and new love that has provided me with hope. To Mason, you 'leapt' forward with inspiration when I needed it most and I look forward to returning the favour one day.

I would not be half the person I am today if not for many of my family members. All those cousins in England and St. Lucia, my cheeky Auntie Nina, my little sisters Inez and Noor, my inspiring dad, Greg and my rock of a brother Raoul. They have ALL contributed to my life offering support, encouragement, many hours of laughter and loads of hugs.

And last but not least, the most heartfelt thanks to my mum, Yvonne. You are my best critic and my strongest supporter. You saw something in me worth believing in long before I believed in myself. You are emotional but a rock, impatient and yet patient, tired but you never stop, calm amid the chaos but most of all, you are simply bloody wonderful Mum.

PHOTOGRAPHIC ACKNOWLEDGEMENTS

THE author and publisher would like to thank the following for permission to reproduce photographs:

Quinn Rooney/Getty Images, Matt King/Stringer/Getty Images, Scott Barbour/Getty Images, Nigel Owen/Action Plus/Getty Images, Michael Dodge/Getty Images

Other photographs are from private collections.

Every reasonable effort has been made to trace the copyright holders, but if there are any errors or omissions, Hodder & Stoughton will be pleased to insert the appropriate acknowledgement in any subsequent printings or editions.